CW01429961

HEAVEN'S ABOVE!

HEAVEN'S ABOVE!

F. M. Kershaw

VANTAGE PRESS
New York

Published by Vantage Press, Inc.
516 West 34th Street, New York, New York 10001

Manufactured in the United States of America
ISBN: 0-533-10231-6

Library of Congress Catalog Card No.: 92-93301

0 9 8 7 6 5 4 3 2 1

To the idea that by a degree of self-discipline, men and women would have attained just that element of freedom which they ardently sought. Now mankind is in bondage to a lust for power, passion, and personal gain.

Contents

Foreword

There are very few books which allow us to really know the author. When reading an autobiography we may sense a closeness to the author in that we are invited to stand alongside at important events in their life, or again when studying a philosophy we may feel close to the writer as we trek the path of understanding set out for us to follow. But these seldom match the dimension of awareness we may gain here.

Heaven's Above! is part biography, part philosophy of life, and most importantly we really meet its author. We learn of ventures undertaken, reasoning concerning the world's problems and the interface between God and man, and most importantly we discover what really makes Frank Kershaw tick.

As a friend of Frank's for a number of years (since chapter 8), my most useful comment on his work is to let you know that the man you meet in these pages really is Frank Kershaw. He invites us to share deep into his life. In his most private moments of anguish and revelation. This is a real person working out his life; it is not a rosy review or an ego trip in any way. It is for real.

Since our first meeting back in 1978 I have regarded Frank as being "his own person." Frank never seems to regard peer pressure and is as much at ease as a minority of one as being part of a smooth majority. The criteria for decision and action are certainly not bound by another's reasoning, yet the activity of his life results from inner promptings and his understanding on observations of life as he has witnessed it. Frank may describe life in terms of "cause and effect" and we can easily understand his reasons and realise the working out of his life is because of an empathy with the cause governing it.

John Castell-Evans

Introduction

When I walked into the bedroom I could feel something was different. My wife was there just as I had left her two minutes before, half sitting up in bed, but there was no response to my query. For nearly fifty years we had very close contact with one another. Now, nothing. It was stunning. Her face had lost what little colour it had, and a thin trickle of saliva issued from the corner of her mouth. The body was there intact, but there was no longer any control, any communication, any life. My wife had died.

I am sure that others must feel as I felt in wanting at that first realization to do all manner of mad things: turn back the clock, shout out loud, even shake that inert form to wake it up.

As a baby her first cry would have heralded the fact that life was there. What had happened now? What fundamental change had taken place?

There were things that had to be done. There was no time therefore to try and come to terms with this climactic event in my life, but later I had to concentrate. Where now was my dear wife? What had really happened? What, in fact, was life all about? All my own ups and downs, trials and tribulations, joys and sorrows—all these were the typical ingredients of the end product but, surely to goodness, this lifeless form could not be the end product?

This demanded an explanation, and that explanation is, to a large extent, the story of my life. From my earliest recollections at about five years old to the most recent events, there is meaning in everything.

How I yearn to impart some of that understanding to those many who have been unable either to comprehend or, if knowing, to accept. Constantly I gather from the media, in its various forms of the spoken word, that the common complaint of mankind is that it can find no meaning to its existence. That I so believe in what I have learned is my only excuse for embarking upon what I recognise as an impudence and which will probably be seen as such by many. It is a matter of belief, when all is said and done. There is, indeed, meaning in the sad fact that so many find it impossible to believe in the goodness of all things. This is a sweeping, paradoxical statement in opposition to the general worldly conception of things, but it is one I intend to defend and attempt to explain.

A Word of Gratitude

I wish to express my thanks and deep appreciation for the willing assistance I have received from:

Mrs. Marion Martyn, who has typed the manuscript and given much other valuable help;

Dr. John Castell-Evans, for his willingness to provide the Foreword;

My daughter, Mrs. Shiela Cherry, for much help, especially in photocopying by her business, Rutland Word Processing.

HEAVEN'S ABOVE!

The Period in Prison as a Conscientious Objector

Since I had no clear idea of what I wanted to do or be except some vague notion of "going up the classical side" at Manchester Grammar School, I am prepared to accept that a broken leg, my sister's infectious illness, and a variety of other small details all combined to send me, at the age of thirteen, "up the modern side." My father's ideas of a safe job in a bank or insurance company were anathema to me, but I had no personal hand in finding myself accepted as a trainee by Exide Batteries or, more correctly, The Chloride Electrical Storage Co., Ltd. That was entirely due to Tommy Ormerod, a master at M.G.S., who must surely have given me a very good reference unbeknown to myself.

Along with another trainee named Kirk, I studied electrical engineering at night school, encouraged by the firm. In my final year two jobs became available, one in India and the other as an accountant at Chloride's Glasgow depot. The company decided that as I was then courting my fiancée I was not the most suitable candidate for India so sent me to Glasgow.

The only practical use to which I ever put six years' study of D.C. motors, alternators, or the construction of the electric line from Manchester to Altrincham was in stage lighting for amateur dramatics. My studies covered the period when pylons were being erected all over the country to carry transmission lines, and I learned how to calculate resistance, impedance, and capacitance effects in these lines. If you see a pylon on a hillside with transmission lines swooping downhill in a beautiful lopsided curve, you will know that someone has wrestled with an equation eighteen inches long to calculate the cable size, distances between cables and between pylons.

Except perhaps as mind training, concentration and such ancillary benefits, I never used a scrap of my knowledge. The period was 1928–1934—the Depression years out of which the country was to emerge into the Hitler era: *The War.*

It is not a matter that for me required any defence. I had never had any doubt that I should be a conscientious objector. It was something inbred, not thought out. It was an internal conviction that brooked no alternative. To glory in the force of arms is so foreign to my nature that when I see films of battles portrayed I experience a mixture of emotions: amazement, disgust, horror amounting to disbelief that human beings can be so barbaric. I can understand to some extent a single individual being gripped by an evil influence, but for whole groups of men to slash and cut and maim their fellow beings in frenzied attacks is astounding.

True, as I consider history, it has been going on for a long time, even getting worse, and always the root causes are the twin sins of greed and envy. If mankind has, despite this, achieved anything, just think what could have been achieved if compassion and cooperation had been the main driving forces.

Needless to say, there were a great many at the start of the 1939 conflict who not only could not agree with me but were very antagonistic, including the members of the tribunal that I was invited to attend.

I was assigned to a noncombatant section, the Royal Engineers, but it was twelve months before I was eventually called up and told to appear in Ilfracombe. I politely wrote to the C.O. advising him that as a conscientious objector or c.o. (slightly ironic, that) I could not voluntarily put in an appearance. In the meantime I made arrangements for my wife and newly born twin daughters to vacate our house in Glasgow to live for the duration of the war with Winifred's parents in Cleveleys, Lancashire. Here I must digress, because I was often asked what I would do if the enemy invaded our shores, if he attacked the town and street where I lived, and what in fact I would do were soldiers to appear at my front door. It begs the question that an unarmed man would have little or no chance to defend his family in those circumstances, because it had already been assumed by those asking the question that at some point I would have decided to fight. This is a fundamental issue.

Taken to its logical conclusion it meant that if I was not prepared to take up arms, then I could not "lift a finger" to save my family. People threw up their hands in horror that a man could be such a coward as to take that view. It was against human nature. Indeed, it is. So is the idea of "turning the other cheek" or of "feeding your enemy." I personally never could see it as cowardice, because it took an immense amount of courage and willpower even to consider the stand. In fact, I realised I was being called upon to sacrifice my family (if need be) for the sake of my convictions, and I was reminded of the story of Abraham being called by God to be prepared to sacrifice Isaac. If anyone thinks that is an easy option, I assure them that I did not find it so. In fact, neither Abraham nor myself had to make the sacrifice—it was sufficient to be wholly prepared to do so.

I shall refer back to this basic truth because I have found it to be a human failing to be unable to face up to the logical consequences of a course of action. Men and women always stop short of the ultimate decision, whether it be in the case of fighting or sex or the cost of an operation. They regard the words of Jesus Christ as hyperbole when He said, "If thine eye offend thee, pluck it out, or if thine arm offend thee, cut it off."

So we have another historical fact. All the way through

My twin daughters, aged four months

My twin daughters, aged four years

history mankind has compromised. Today, in his efforts to unravel the tangled web of compromise, he has to endeavour to make decisions on genetic experiments, abortion, and many other matters.

So it turned out, my letter to the commanding officer having set in motion a chain of reactions, that as I sat in front of a bright coal fire reading Dickens's *Christmas Carol* on Christmas Eve 1940 there came a knock at the door. Two policeman stood there with instructions to pick me up and take me to the gaol in Blackpool. There I spent three nights because there was no court till the 27th of December to remand me into the custody of the army.

I was sustained physically and mentally by two dozen mince pies baked by my wife. This told me that we were together in whatever lay before us. For her it was weeks of uncertainty while looking after two six-month-old babies. For me, a brief outline of events will, I hope, be of interest. When the military took charge, I was put in a makeshift cell at the end of a large, first floor room, which had been used for cold storage. It still was a cold place! There was a broken window in my cell and a board to lie on. My coat and blanket were taken away, and a cold northwesterly wind blew straight in. Curiously, I recall no particular discomfort.

After a week I was taken under armed guard to Ilfracombe and billeted in a small hotel commandeered for the job. For several days I received almost V.I.P. treatment and the best of Christmas fare, I suspect in an endeavour to persuade me that the army wasn't so bad after all. This was one of several instances indicating that the authorities had not the slightest idea of what conscientious objection was all about. Next, I found myself in a small room with sixteen others and a bucket. For the first time in my life I was with others who shared my convictions and with whom I could converse in like terms. Nevertheless, on one occasion I spent five hours squatting on the floor talking to one man on what we each meant by "faith." With almost anyone it is necessary to spend a long while in order to establish an identity of thought.

Up till now I had no contact with anyone other than Methodists, and only one particular church. I listened with rapt attention to the views of Pentecostals, Plymouth Brethren, Christadelphians, Church of England, Latter Day Saints, British Israelites, and Congregationalists, to mention a few. In due course, each of us received an order which, needless to say, was not obeyed. Punishment was up to one month in a military detention prison (Shepton Mallett to be exact). Here the guards were not allowed to administer physical punishment but resorted to a number of "accidents." The favourite was accidentally to trip you at the top of a flight of seven concrete steps.

As everyone knows, everything in a detention barracks is done at the double. In the space of five weeks I had thirty-two stripped examinations, only two of which I could regard as in any way official, the rest were "for fun."

Back at base, the situation became awkward for both the military and ourselves. Those in charge quickly realised that given an order we would refuse but asked politely we always obliged. We were getting requests instead of orders. Fortunately the question for myself was soon resolved, because I was transferred to Huyton, near Liverpool, and sufficiently close to Cleveleys (whither my family had moved for the duration) for me to hitchhike there, letting the commanding officer know what I had done. This act incurred a civil prison sentence of ninety-one days, and I soon found myself in the then warm and comfortable Walton Prison—but only for a week. Along with approximately thirty other prisoners, I was removed, handcuffed to another prisoner, in a motor coach to Stafford Prison. I think it worth mentioning that with only one bucket filled to overflowing, emptying the bladder while handcuffed to someone else in a bumpety coach is a hazardous performance, but not lethal.

Stafford was run on military lines, and because it was considered that I might "contaminate" other prisoners I was kept in almost solitary confinement, not even being allowed to mend post office mailbags in company with others. I had to repair my quota in my own cell. Prison clothing was all wool and warm, thank goodness, because there seemed to be no heat on at Stafford. Even today I have relatively poor circulation in my legs and feet so, of course, my feet are usually cold. This was certainly the case in prison, but I had an inspiration: the rope edging on the mailbags was thick and I stitched up a pair of warm slippers. These I dutifully put out with the rest of my "kit"—plate, mug, knife, fork, spoon, and blanket—for daily inspection. The warder came along. "What the —— are these?" says he. I explained that I suffered from cold feet. "I'll say you do," said the warder, knowing well that I was a c.o. Surprise, surprise, he let me keep them.

All meals were rationed. I think four ounces of bread, a half ounce of butter, and a half ounce of sugar were supplied in what to me looked like cut-down shell cartridges. The prison-baked bread, fresh every day, was delicious. The sugar didn't matter to me, but the butter ration was quite inadequate. Each meal was brought round by prisoners accompanied by a warder, and theoretically one could take one's pick—but not I. I was given the smallest by the warder. Icelandic salted cod was often on the menu and my share was always the black tail-end. I lived. One way in which I helped myself was to allow the four o'clock mug of cocoa to go cold. A quarter of an inch of fat solidified on the top and handsomely augmented my butter ration.

At four o'clock you were left alone, entirely unmolested till 6:00 A.M., and immediately after my meal I squatted cross-legged on my board; hard labour, which I was given, meant no palliass. I did not know it at the time but I was adopting the yogi position for contemplation and I found myself quite able to lose myself in meditation, oblivious of all things except my thoughts for the next four hours. I had a confusion of many thoughts about God, Jesus Christ, religion in all its forms, and of course, my own position as a conscientious objector.

It seemed that my upbringing as a Methodist had done very little to help me understand the verities of the Bible; indeed, even now, fifty years later, I am discovering truths I never knew existed when I was thirty. Listening to the other conscientious objectors of quite different religions but still Christians, I had picked up and retained many ideas that were new to me. Such a welter of ideas, but none helped much towards enlightenment of my present situation. I was a conscientious objector by reason of an inner conviction, not by mental argument. I knew I could not have joined the Army Medical Corps, but I could not explain why to the many who saw no reason except cowardice for my aversion. I had been given "noncombatant" status by the tribunal; why could I not accept that? At that moment I couldn't even give myself a satisfactory reason, let alone others.

One thing in the church to which I had belonged troubled me greatly. It was all right to sing hymns or pray about Jesus Christ at a service in the church, but to my concern any mention of His name outside the church, in ordinary conversation, always caused an embarrassed silence, even in my own home. There was something wrong here, thought I, but—brainwashed as I had been by standard Methodist teaching and thinking—it was very difficult to thread one's way through the labyrinth of thoughts that the situation provoked. To my relief it had not been a difficulty amongst the c.o.'s at the barracks. Jesus was spoken of freely. This at least gave me a lead.

There was another factor that worried me. The Methodist Conference had discussed pacifism and had decided it could give no guide on the matter. The question was to be left entirely to the individual. At the time this was for me an inconvenience, since I was without the church's backing at my tribunal, whereas some others had that backing. In time it became obvious that the strictures in Revelation 4 relating to the church of the Laodiceans was true of Methodism as a whole but not necessarily of individuals in the church. Over the years I regret I have had no reason to change my opinion on this. It is one thing to have had a lifetime of experience on these matters, but something quite different to be faced with this and so many questions of a like nature in one's formative years.

I now see clearly and believe without a shadow of doubt that God knew all about it—knew that it was needful for me to have gone through this route involving military discipline and a prison sentence rather than for me to go direct onto the land. I rejoice and praise God for His goodness in so leading me. At the time I was in a veritable quagmire of seemingly unrelated thoughts and doubts.

This, then, was the position when I found myself able to throw off the world and concentrate solely on trying to unravel the tangle. What a blessing to be able to do this continuously for five or six weeks without impediment of any sort.

The culminating blessing was treasure indeed! Three weeks before the end of my sentence a curious thing happened. I was escorted by a warder to church on the Sunday morning. Why this had never happened before, I do not know. To say that it was not to my liking would be a gross understatement. It was hateful. Incense swinging and genuflecting are repugnant to me. When, therefore, on the following Sunday my door was unlocked and the warder proceeded to take me to church I prayed urgently to be excused and return to my cell. How it happened I do not know, but suddenly I found myself quite alone on the landing and was able to return to my cell. I left the door open and, lifting up my gaze to heaven, gave heartfelt thanks to Almighty God. "God is a Spirit and they that worship Him must worship Him in Spirit and in Truth."

All forms of physical expression mitigate against worship. Solitude and quietness are the key. So I stood alone in my cell at twenty-one minutes past ten o'clock on the 23rd of March 1941, giving thanks to God, and the whole cell filled with brilliant cool light. I was enveloped in it for about four seconds, and my life was changed. Tears streamed down my face. It was ecstasy.

It was as though the myriad pieces of a broken mirror suddenly rushed together and formed a perfect whole. And I knew with absolute certainty that I now had someone as a guide who would help to control my actions and decisions for the rest of my life. All those many problems and questions fell into place, and I found myself with convictions on a number of matters where there had previously been confusion.

On such matters as prayer: Why does God not always answer prayer? I have a clear, concise understanding. Why serious accidents? Why are small children allowed to suffer and die? On suffering generally I have no doubts about the reason and the value. Not that I realised all the answers on this one morning, but the road to the answers was clearly indicated and is the reason why I have embarked on writing this book. Not that in any way I consider myself specially equipped, but some matters are of perennial interest and most people do not seem to have a clue.

The most immediate answer that presented itself was, fairly naturally, that concerning conscientious objection. When I think of how demoralised I once felt and now how simple the answer was, I am both amazed and amused. It was so obvious that I could participate in any work that was undertaken in peacetime, but not in those operations that were a direct result of the country being at war. To be set to work clearing and digging drainage ditches was quite acceptable.

Form whatever opinion you like on the next paragraph; I have no answer as to how, but a very precise understanding of why!

It seemed to me that I had to get down in writing some expression of what had just happened, and my new-found convictions, and I had the means. Up till now we had been allowed a pen and ink for no more than one hour once a month for a letter home, but since I had forms to fill in relative to my impending second tribunal, the rule had been relaxed and I had use of pen and ink for quite some time. Moreover, I had copies of the forms and was able to use the back for the purpose of writing my "catechism." I quickly filled three pages. I seem to recollect reading through what I had put down, but never saw the papers again. Not even a warder visited my cell, so what happened to the three sheets I have no idea, but their disappearance had a profound effect. I realised then what has since been many times confirmed: that one should not try to pin down the Holy Spirit of God. It is *ongoing*—then, now, and at all times. What is right for today is not necessarily right tomorrow. The Spirit that moves through the world and through men and women is fluid, not static. This is well illustrated by the comments of the Lord to the Pharisees when He reminded them of how David went into the temple and ate the shewbread (Mark 2:24–28).

From this moment onwards I was a happy man. The pinpricks and restrictions of prison life no longer bothered me, and in any case I knew I had only a fortnight to go before my tribunal and release.

The tribunal was to be held at Ebury House, and for the last week I was moved to Wandsworth Prison for easy transportation in the London area. I well remember my first night in a reception cell at Wandsworth. I had heard of bed bugs, but never seen any. Here I encountered thousands. They were everywhere, little red beetles like squashed ladybirds and just as colourful. I hate killing any of God's creatures, but I just had to scoop up and dispose of loads of these before I could think of lying down. I shared my bed that night with hundreds of them.

The tribunal went according to expectations and I was ordered to report to the Lancashire War Agricultural Committee. You will recall that I had moved my family for the duration from Glasgow to Cleveleys, Lancashire, to the home of my wife's parents, so Lancashire was to be my sphere of operations. My two daughters were one year old.

Two Miracles Start Me in Business

I was billeted to begin with in a hostel and taken each day to Southern Heyes, a swampy area of peat near Formby. Here I spent each day kebbing out ditches. A kebb is a curved hay fork type of instrument, and after the first half hour I was exhausted. After three months, however, I could handle the tools continuously for a whole day with very few pauses and only feel pleasantly tired at day's end. It was for me a new and exhilarating experience to have such stamina.

Life at the hostel was pleasant enough; the rooms were adequate and I never had any complaints about food. I was hungry enough to tackle anything. An accomplished musician created a choral society which I joined. I cherish the memory of learning the whole of the *Messiah*, which we sang in the Gaumont picture theatre in Chorley. Isabel Bailey, Kathleen Ferrier, and Owen Brannigan were three of the soloists. I apologise to the tenor for having forgotten his name.

Shortly after this I was moved to a different hostel at Aughton, near Ormskirk. I was made foreman of one of four gangs that went throughout south Lancashire visiting farms to put in field drainage. On a given field the outlet at the lowest point would be agreed and a hole dug by hand. Into this a type of plough was lowered, which was then towed by a steel cable on a drum operated by a tractor at the upper limit of the trench. It cut a continuous ribbon of earth ten inches wide and twelve inches deep—continuous, that is, so long as you hit no boulders, as happened quite often. The operation was performed twice, giving a trench two feet deep; and on the bottom

14

Laying field-drainage tiles

cut a shoe was attached to take out a shallow, four-inch-wide segment. This formed the bed for the four-inch clay field drain pipes, which were placed in and the earth returned. Undoubtedly this was the basic ground work on which the future peacetime increase of farm produce in this country was planned and executed.

It was while stationed at Hutton that eight of us spent a couple of hours one evening a week in an experiment which to myself was most salutory. One of our number introduced us to the idea of contacting the spirit world. Four of us sat at a smooth table on which the letters of the alphabet had been placed round the perimeter. A small upturned glass was placed in the middle. When we each placed a finger over the glass—and I stress *over* because we did not touch the glass—it would move. Again I emphasise that the glass was not being pushed. I have learned since that this is the principle of the Ouija board. To me it demonstrated emphatically that there was a power outside ourselves. When I have told would-be Christians about this experiment they have thrown up their hands in horror. Dabbling with evil spirits—shocking!

I did not regard myself as doing anything sinful. I was merely finding out how far the mechanics of this phenomenon would take us. It was largely played as a game, but a serious game. We always insisted that we contact only good guides because, for one thing, if you did not the result was unintelligible. The efficacy of the system relied on our concentration to provide the power, and regularly we were exhorted to CONCENTRATE. Obviously, each of us would ask questions, the answers to which were unknown to the others. Perhaps it would be the age of so-and-so, or his or her address. Very simple stuff but illuminating none the less. If we ever asked a question to reveal the future we were told it was not within the province of our contact to answer.

Indeed, I came to the conclusion that we are all of us

subject throughout our lives to good and bad influences, and it is not necessary to resort to Ouija, which can do no more than the influences about us; but we do react to them every hour of our lives. We were informed that every person at birth had twelve guides assigned, both good and bad. A bad guide in a person can easily be seen by most of us because it results in him or her having a bad habit. For the most part one would need to have a very good understanding of human psychology to appreciate the significance of some of our traits. For instance I was told that I had two faulty guides, one resulting in pride and the other in sarcasm, and that part of life's meaning was for us to get rid of the guide that caused the trait and have it replaced by a better one. I find nothing very revolutionary in that. Nor can I say that I was surprised to find that one bad guide, which caused "too much setting of seed," was in opposition to the one that caused pride.

That I had both traits was evident to me if not to others. Indeed I was shocked that often in my prayers I felt a shadow of resentment cross through me that anyone, even Jesus Himself, could be preferred above me. I do not need to be told how silly and sinful such a thought is, but knowing that did not prevent the thought from recurring regularly. The exigencies of life have taught me to think differently, and forty years on I am no longer troubled by such wilfulness. That is again proof that we are all under influences that have profound effects on us. Paul put it perfectly: "We wrestle not against flesh and blood but against principalities and powers, against the rulers of the darkness of this world, against spiritual wickedness in high places" (Eph. 6:12).

That the movement of the glass was not caused by some little-understood psychology or psyche or other occult power within us expressing itself was one day very clearly exemplified—to us at any rate. We had become accustomed to finding either one of two guides at our service and were

17

surprised on this occasion to find a new guide in attendance. We had opened the meeting in the usual manner by one of us silently asking a question. The rest of us could not only *not* know the answer until it was given, but we couldn't even know the question. After receiving an answer it was usual for us to say "thank you." Immediately the glass spelt out P-R-A-E-G-O. To all of us this was unintelligible and the guide was asked to repeat the spelling. None of us knew at the time that this was common Italian practice in conversation, to acknowledge the thanks. The French do it, the Germans say "Bitte." Even the British are sometimes polite enough to say something like "my pleasure" or "don't mention it." It transpired on this occasion that our new guide had been a guide to Caruso, the famous tenor, and had become accustomed to the usage. He told us also that he had been a guide to Xerxes, the Syrian king.

One other point before I leave this subject. When British people ask a question of anyone they more often than not say, "Can you tell me? . . . " The correct answer to that question is either "Yes, I can" or "No, I cannot." Those are precisely the answers we always got, so we then had to say "Please tell us . . ." A useful lesson in the correct use of language.

Referring to influences affecting our lives, I am reminded that before I was married my father and mother, my fiancée, and myself used to enjoy playing contract bridge on a Saturday night. I became more and more convinced that there was a pattern to the way the cards fell to the players. It was not just chance, because chance is indiscriminate and I felt strongly that there was an influence behind the way the cards fell. I do not doubt that most people will "pooh, pooh" such an idea, and I confess I have never had the time or inclination to look deeply into it. Suffice it to say that today and for a long time when watching football, snooker, or tennis on television I have often remarked to myself that "that team" or "that person" will lose, "the fates are against them." I have seldom been wrong.

Once, the team I was working with discussed over lunch in a barn the different weights of individuals they knew. I was not present at the start of the conversation, and when I joined them the question was shot at me: Frank, how heavy do you think so-and-so is? Right off the top of my head and without thinking about it I gave a figure. They were surprised that I was only half an ounce out, and of course suggested someone else. Again I replied without thought and was again surprisingly close. By the time they put the question again I had begun to think—think, too, how clever I was. On this third occasion I was far, far out, because self had entered the equation.

Training of course plays a large part in any human being's achievement, but it affects the level at which a result is achieved, not the result itself. The world talks a lot about confidence and pressures. All will agree that when watching an individual perform any activity confidence or the lack of it, i.e., nerves, quite evidently affects the result. "Metaphysical influences," largely unsuspected and little understood, are the deciding factors at any given moment in one's life.

It is obvious that winning or losing a tournament has a pronounced effect on a person's life at that moment, but if he or she pauses to ask the question *why*, the answer will almost invariably be in physical, observable, human terms. Few people will question the condition of their souls or, if you prefer the word, psyches. Not too many people are concerned about vague terms, even if they are aware of them. I shall have to return to consideration of such matters from time to time throughout these pages, for they bring us gradually to the ultimate, vital conviction about life itself.

In the meantime, however, let us return to more mundane but equally important matters. For perhaps eighteen months during 1941 and 1942 I was using a bicycle to get either to work or to the nearest railway station. Those who are old enough will no doubt remember that if you travelled on the train before 7:30 A.M. or after 5:00 P.M. (I am open to correction on the exact times) you were entitled to use a workman's ticket. Again I am not sure of the precise figures, but I think I am fairly safe in saying that you could cover over five miles with a ticket for 1/6 (one shilling and sixpence) or seven and a half pence in today's currency. It was also true that you could walk on and off a station without even showing your ticket; there was no one there to check it. I found myself with a pocketful of tickets, and, since no one ever bothered to look at the date, I hit on the idea of using one ticket to get on a station and a different one to exit, having covered a much larger distance than either ticket allowed for. I did not regard this as "sharp practice" but as "good business." How many things in life are differentiated between by those two terms!

To get back to the bicycle. I used to chain it up at the departure station to await my return. I was slightly annoyed, therefore, when my hand pump disappeared, but I quickly replaced it. When the second one vanished I felt vaguely that I was being told something, but it was not until my camera (my prize possession) was stolen—and, please note, from a compartment of a railway coach—that I began seriously to consider the situation. The first thing to occur to me was the connection of these losses with the railway, and it was only a short step to link that fact with the quite obvious one that I was defrauding the railway company by my manipulation of the tickets. I stopped at once and have lost nothing more by theft up to this day.

I accepted then, and fifty years later am convinced, that a principle applies throughout human relationships that if you steal, something will be taken from you. The same applies if you defraud anyone. Using office paper clips renders you liable to lose something of equivalent value. I used to take pleasure in re-using stamps that had missed the franking machine. I received one such the other day but I will not use it. This may seem a very little thing but it is axiomatic. Indeed, one must be prepared to go still further. If for instance you receive more than the right amount of change, instead of walking gleefully away you must reveal the error and have it corrected. Would not life be much pleasanter if we could rely on all people to do thus?

(Two years after I had ceased the practice of manipulating tickets a man was apprehended by railway security men, stealing two pounds of rhubarb. When his premises were searched my camera was found with a Glasgow address attached, and after some considerable wandering it was returned to me, but the film packs that made it such a versatile instrument were no longer available.)

Three years passed, during which time thousands of acres of poorish land were drained and brought into production from the Mersey to the Lune and from the Pennines to the Fylde coast, and I was feeling physically fit. I had, however, observed a lot of waste, particularly of expensive machinery, and when a meeting of foremen was called I found myself giving a speech in which I enumerated several instances. Within a fortnight I was sacked.

Several other changes were taking place at about the same time. The Allied Forces were advancing in Europe and there was a more relaxed feeling abroad. Lancashire did not have to suffer the trauma of "doodle-bugs" as did London. By now I had become convinced that baptism by immersion was not only desirable but basic to a real Christian faith. A friend of mine, Jim Callaghan, was very hopeful that I would accept his suggestion that his church in Wallasey would be available for the ceremony, but I saw no urgency until one morning while I was staying with my sister near Manchester. Now unemployed, I was lying in bed contemplating the future with particular reference to my own desire to go on my own. Cutting right across these thoughts I heard a voice speak to me as clearly as if someone had been standing by the bed. It said, "I can do no more for you until you are baptised." In a flash I was out of bed and on the telephone to the pastor of the Wallasey church, wanting to be baptised that very evening. The event actually took a fortnight to arrange, and to my great delight my wife, Winifred, joined me. Mr. Hulse in his sermon made it clear that following baptism people should not be surprised to find themselves tempted and tested, and so it was with me and mine.

On the meaning and origin of baptism, this seems an appropriate point at which to pause and consider. Nowhere in the Bible is there a specific command on the subject, but the inference is very strong. John the Baptist baptised in the Jordan "where there was much water." His baptism was a call to repentance of sins, and he demurred when Jesus Himself presented Himself for baptism. Jesus said to him, "Suffer it to be so now, for thus it becometh us to fulfil all righteousness" (Matt. 3:15). Let us note that the temptation of Jesus followed immediately upon his baptism. Then there is the beautiful story of Philip and the Ethiopian eunuch, totally nonplussed on reading in Isaiah how Jesus Christ was to be treated. When Philip had explained and they had come near to water, the eunuch said, "What doth hinder me to be baptised." And Philip said, "If thou believest with all thy heart, thou mayest." The eunuch replied, "I believe that Jesus Christ is the Son of God." "They went down into the water together and Philip baptised him" (Acts 8:26–39).

It should be noted here that there is a difference, an important difference, between the baptism of John, which signified repentance of sins, and the baptism of believers, which demonstrates the participant's confession of faith that Jesus Christ is the Son of God, and our Lord and Saviour.

This is the heart of the matter and the point on which the early church soon went astray. Around the years 210 to 230 a dispute arose between the Carthaginian Bishop Tertullian and

Bishop Origen. The latter had become concerned that so many young people died before being baptised, and Origen felt it necessary to baptise earlier and earlier. Tertullian dissented and tried to keep the emphasis on confession of faith. Notwithstanding, the concern for children and babies—many of whom in those days died in infancy—grew until it became accepted custom that children should be "baptised" as soon as possible after birth. I put *baptised* in inverted commas because, coincidental with early baptism, it was obvious that immersion was inappropriate for babies. Splashing with water was much more efficacious. Thus the whole *raison d'être* of baptism was turned upside down. The christening of a baby was given more importance than the confession of faith, which was the reason for it. As has happened so often in the history of the church, religion went completely off the rails and for the most part has never got back on.

Taking the line of least resistance has all too often resulted in a dilution of intent; expediency has dictated action. This is so much the case in the present day, not only in matters of faith but even more in secular concerns, that people have lost sight of the principles of right and wrong. I must not digress too far, but consider the arguments on sex, divorce, marriage, embryos, and abortion, to name but a few. A whole chapter can be written on each.

I had practically been told to be baptised, and I fairly joyfully complied, but it is not very easy. After all, one does not normally have a bath in public, and it takes a certain amount of determination. It also demands meekness, in the first place because, as Baptists recognise it, it implies being buried with Christ, and in the second place because it means submission to another person.

So my wife and I were baptised and, as I have said, other things were changing. I was free of the Lancashire War Agricultural Committee but not, of course, of government direction.

The latter did not inhibit change of address, and we were having to leave Cleveleys. Since our rented house in Glasgow had been sublet and now came empty just when we wanted it, we returned to Glasgow.

Remember that I was unemployed and wanted to work for myself. I did not apply for unemployment pay, though I had to be registered. God had promised to supply all my needs and I believed He would. He did. I had £150 in the bank and an aunt of Winifred's she had lost touch with left us £150 in her will. This was totally unexpected as I say, but exactly needful. I did not accept unemployment pay on another count; i.e., I had not been prepared to fight and I did not consider it right to expect the country to keep me now. In fact, I never accepted child benefit either.

A passage of scripture not infrequently occurred to me relative to all matters as between one's duty to God and that to one's country: I Samuel, chapter 8, verses 11–18. I am bound to comment that in 1992 everyone seemingly expects the government to cure all ills, something which it is patently unable to do, for as fast as it attempts to solve one problem it usually creates two more. When God is believed, when God is trusted and waited for without our interfering, the result is wonderful and perfect. I was about to have a salutory lesson in patience.

How blessed was I to have a wife who not only saw things in much the same way but had the strength of character to go along with all the vicissitudes. Make no mistake about it, this was to be a test and a trial indeed, far greater than I could envisage at that moment. We started the first months in high spirits. We were together again as a family in our first home and I believed God was about to show His power by starting me in business on my own. I had no clear idea of what I wanted to do but had achieved a limited success before the war as a children's photographer and freelance journalist. The first month passed and I was sent to apply for a job with a local horticulturist. He didn't want me. Another month passed and I was told to apply to another concern with the same result. I was not unduly concerned, however, as I still felt the strong assurance that God would do something wonderful. I felt that I must be patient and be prepared to wait, say, six months, but six months went by and three or four visits to firms were to prove abortive.

One morning when the post arrived with another appointment I was happily engaged in making myself a portable rack for holding a variety of tools, and I was most unwilling to leave this and go on this errand. The way in which I suddenly lost my balance and fell onto the half-made rack was most peculiar. My handiwork was ruined. That, to me, was a sign of God's displeasure, and I immediately departed to visit the firm. No job resulted, but I learned that I must keep to the rules without demur. So six, seven, eight, nine months passed with only one noticeable change in my circumstances. There were no signs or indications of any sort of job, least of all one in which I could be my own boss; the only change was in my bank balance, which was now down to half. Things were beginning to get a little trying. We were spending as a family about four pounds a week, and I began to think it was time something showed up. My wife was as staunch as ever, but a further four months slipped by and I was beginning to feel fretful at times. I was never bored; there was always something to occupy myself with. Just down the road was a small sawmill, the owner of which gave me permission to use a circular saw for cutting up logs, which I then chopped up for firewood and hawked round the district. What I got in cash was negligible, but it felt good to be able to do something. I am horrified when I recall that saw. It was two feet in diameter with wicked-looking teeth that revolved at high speed. It was suspended above the bench and counter-balanced so that you could draw it towards you, position the log, and then let the saw swing back, slicing through the wood like a knife through butter. All the time I used it I had a horrid picture of what that saw could do to an arm or a hand in a split second. It was very dangerous.

I was spending more and more time in prayer on my knees; not that I was saying much. My period in prison when I had spent so much time in meditation had taught me not to waste time before God in vain words, but just to contemplate in awe His majesty and remain quietly submissive to His will. Nevertheless, on one occasion I went far into the night in what was something very similar to Jacob's experience when he wrestled with an angel. I know that I had a question put to me: "What do you wish that I should do for you?" "Lord," I said, "that I might have faith and be able to do things for myself."

Nothing apparently happened, and life went on as before. We were now into the fourteenth month of unemployment, resources very much depleted and still no sign of an end. True, the war was over, but I was still under direction and had been to eight different appointments for a job. Whenever I was sent to a market gardener or horticultural firm, I wondered if it could be that I might obtain training for setting up later on my own, but the prospective employer did not see things that way. I am sure they thought to themselves, "This chap isn't the right type; he knows nothing. The war is over and we don't want to spend time and money training someone."

I kept asking myself, When is something going to happen? and even occasionally, Should I be taking some action for myself? This latter idea I quickly ruled out. Not only was it against the divine principle, "O, rest in the Lord, wait patiently for Him," but I knew that if what I might do should result in my getting a job, I could never be sure that I was doing what God intended. That would undermine my confidence. Waiting patiently for God is fundamental; it is basic. One must be sure of God's will and that means absolutely no interference on my part.

I cannot stress this too much in view of the prevailing human sentiments that "God helps those who help themselves" and "If you pray for something, don't just stand around waiting for it, get moving." There are more illustrations of a like sentiment that will spring to mind, and they are all flawed, badly flawed. I've heard preachers advocating action and then announce the next hymn, "Trust and Obey." The Bible all the way through emphasises our need to pray and trust God. Mankind finds this too difficult to accept. Mankind is too impatient. It says to itself, God isn't listening, and gives up.

Well, it isn't easy; it is not intended to be easy. God has a right to be sure of our trust and loyalty, and we, His creatures, should delight to prove it. I write this not just out of a heartfelt certainty but as a result of personal experience—after sixteen months and trips to nine appointments yielding no result, money almost gone and my wife and two little girls to feed. Again and again I had to remind myself of God's Promise: "Seek ye first the Kingdom of God and all these things will be added unto you." "Take no thought for the morrow, what ye shall eat or what ye shall drink, or wherewithal ye shall be clothed . . . for your Heavenly Father knoweth ye have need of all these things." They are words that sound quite different when you read them sitting warm, well fed, and comfortable in church, from when you have been waiting on God sixteen months and then, literally, don't know how to pay the next rent.

A letter from the Bureau arrived. I cannot remember the exact words, but they were something like, "You are directed to present yourself on Monday next to the forestry commission in Strachur, Loch Eck. They are prepared to employ you."

Confusion of thought: I'm trapped; Well, at least I'll be getting a wage; Where the heck is Loch Eck? How do I get there? This is a job but certainly not one in which I shall be working

27

for myself. Is God listening? Has He heard my plea? Am I deluding myself? What a jumble, and all with a growing, nagging doubt about my hopes and aspirations. Urgent prayer was called for, during which all the old assurances came flooding in. Trust, wait, be patient. In all things acknowledge God and obey. Obey—well, yes, I still had to do that because I was still under government direction. So off I went on the Monday morning in spring 1945, surprised at how calm I felt, how fairly sure I was that God would still undertake. I must pause, however, to explain that my father had died at his home in north Manchester and the car that he had taken over when I was "called up," but in which Winifred and I had a large share, reverted to me at about this time. So, given the necessary petrol coupons, I had the means of transport to and from at weekends. What a lovely journey it was, too: from Balloch, up the west side of Loch Lomond to Tarbert, over to Arrochar on Loch Long and up Glencloe and Rest and Be Thankful, and down Glen Kinglas to the north end of Loch Fyne. A short distance down the south east side of Loch Fyne brings you to Strachur. I was directed to what is known in Scotland as a "bothy," a simple wooden construction divided into cubicles for sleeping quarters, a dining area, and a kitchen.

There were seven of us and a chap who acted as cook and washer-up. The rest of us were on the job at 7:30 A.M., wet or fine, leaving in a rowing boat with an outboard motor from a small jetty close to the bothy and crossing to the mountainside on the other side of Loch Eck. The foreman in charge met us there and allocated the day's work.

We carried spruce saplings, Norwegian and Sitka spruce, in baskets slung from our shoulders to about fifteen hundred feet up the hillside. There, with a hay knife (a heavy blade such as farmers used for slicing chunks of hay from the stack), which we plunged into the wet, peaty soil, we prepared the ground for planting. It was a simple but heavy job to yank on the shaft till a large, wet sod was upturned on the ground. The little hillock thus formed provided a suitable and secure base for the saplings to be planted into, at about three feet apart. (I returned two years ago, after forty-five years. The saplings we had planted had grown into full trees, been felled and the land cleared, and the area was returning to its natural state.)

How good it was to be working in the open air in such delectable surroundings and be fit enough to easily climb up and down the hillside several times a day with fresh supplies of spruce saplings. It was one of nature's smallest creatures that on occasion put us all to rout. On certain days the midges would come out in hundreds of thousands and make life unbearable. Even the hardened old foreman gave up. He sat down on the turf, pulled his cape over his head and sat in the smoke of his pipe. We others tried to protect ourselves with anti-midge cream or citronella. The latter was effective but did not last too long, and made you smell like a barrel of lemons. It was a good thing that attacks of midges rarely lasted more than a couple of hours.

At the end of six enjoyable weeks I received two letters. One was from a friend of my War Agriculture days, asking if I would be interested in a partnership with him making tiled fireplaces; the other was from the government releasing me from direction. I was free to go my own way, and at the same time a door had opened.

I was, of course, free to carry on with the Forestry Commission and indeed was warmly invited to do so. I had a decision to make. The outdoor life and interesting work appealed to me greatly, but I had to think of the family, especially my wife. Work with the Forestry Commission meant that for many years we would need to live in isolated environments, and I just could not think of my wife with a bachelor of science degree finding this sufficient to keep her mind occupied or sufficient social life to make life pleasant enough. And there was schooling for my young daughters to consider.

The alternative was a totally unknown path. Albert Foster, who had written to me, had some slight knowledge of making tiled fireplaces from before the war and, more importantly, had contacts with the one or two firms left in the tile-making business. Practically all had been forced to close at the commencement of the war and their premises used for other purposes. Albert and I had appealed to each other, and our philosophy on life generally was close, although he would never claim to be religious. Indeed he was one who could not think of God in a personal sense but only as a motive force. I had two weeks to make up my mind, one of which I spent with the commission and the other with Albert and his wife, Dorothy.

I arrived in Accrington with 16s. 4½d. in my pocket and nothing in the bank, but I was clear in my objectives. I said, "If God intends me to accept this proposition I expect Him to indicate such by providing me with a house while I am staying in Accrington this week."

Houses after six years of war were hard to get. Dorothy said, "You'd better start looking in the paper for adverts."

"No," I said. "I do not propose to take any action myself unless I get some outside encouragement."

"Well," said Dorothy, very forthrightly, "I've never heard anything so daft in all my life." Dorothy was an ardent member of Cannon Street Baptist church. Then she said, "If I look for you and find something, will you follow it up?"

"Yes," I said without hesitation. "That would be fine."

For several years my family had travelled north to Durham at Easter, where my uncle had a quarry. They were wonderful days at Saltersgate on the Durham fells. Saltersgate consisted of eight cottages in a row, standing on the side of a valley, foursquare to the elements. There was no road or pavement either back or front, though a path of sorts linked the back entrances. The bottom cottage was occupied by the Fenwick estates gamekeeper. Next to it an employee at the quarry. Then two cottages knocked into one were occupied by my aunt and uncle. Three cottages above them were occupied by estate workers or quarry men, and the top house had been made into a chapel. Some two hundred yards higher up the fell side ran a single-line railway track. A tarmac road finished on the other side of the railway, having come some two miles from the junction with the Tow Law–Consett road.

How I delighted in the sheer rustic primitiveness of the place and the close proximity of nature. The fell side sloped away from the cottages down to the river a quarter of a mile down in the valley bottom, and from the cottages one looked over to the wide expanse of fell country on the other side with Bean Forest a major focal point. A stream running past the houses at a short distance had been tapped to provide running water, at least in my uncle's property. Lighting was provided by Tilley lamps (vapourised paraffin under pressure). Each house had a front and back garden. Part of the fell side was stoney ground and one had to tread carefully to avoid the eggs of curlews amongst the stones. A small pool formed by the stream had a sandy bank in which numerous sand martins had nested. Oh, the nostalgia for those heavenly visits, especially the fortnight I spent in my early teens, going out almost every day with the gamekeeper. I was introduced to rabbits, badgers' setts, stoats, weasels, and on one occasion an adder, Britain's only poisonous snake. Cottages, railway, quarry, and forest have now all gone.

Always we had to pass through Haslingden, and always someone in the car would exclaim, "Who would want to live in a place like this?" It could have been a beautiful place and still perform its function as a cotton town, but Victorian lack of imagination and love of making money had turned it into a drab greystone wall of a place. The back-to-back dwellings and those built into the hillside with only one outlet to the fresh air (I'm glad to say they have all been done away with) were an outrage on society.

It was therefore with mixed feelings that I agreed to follow up a lead that Dorothy had found in the local paper: an advertisement on Wednesday for Tap Stone House, Hudhey, Haslingden. I knew as I walked up the drive that this house had been reserved for me. It was and still is a large old house standing in its own grounds. Originally built in 1593, a fact testified to by the date carved on the stonework of the south gable, which also bears the initials R.D., the house was too much to cope with for the elderly couple that had been living there. They were asking two thousand pounds. The house had a large, wood-panelled dining-room, a panelled hall, a good-sized sitting-room with two windows plus a French window to the garden, a kitchen, and a morning room. The walls were twenty inches thick, constructed of two stone-built skins with rubble between. Upstairs there was more than ample space on the landing, which had a large skylight; three good-sized bedrooms (the main one being above the sitting-room and measuring twenty feet by fourteen feet); a separate toilet with washbasin; and the bathroom, which had obviously once been a bedroom, now having a bath in the middle of the room.

At the foot of the wide, shallow staircase and at the end of the hallway opposite the front door was a built-up doorway. This had been a connecting door to the servants' quarters, and a much steeper stairway was positioned on the opposite side of the wall adjacent to that in the house proper. Here were two rooms downstairs and two up, and this whole part of the building had its own front and back doors, and provided a separate dwelling called the Cottage. As I have said, I knew inwardly that this was where I would live, but I didn't clinch the deal on the spot. For one thing, I had no money; but the

Tap Stone House

Lord who satisfies all our needs was ready. I mentioned a little earlier that my father had died, and on that Thursday I learned that probate had been announced. My father had divided his estate between my sister and myself with the proviso that we should pay interest at the market rate to our mother for as long as she lived. Surely that was an excellent arrangement, for we each had two thousand pounds in cash exactly, with rents from two lots of properties in Blackley and Gorton, Manchester. Negotiations were quickly concluded and arrangements made for us to remove from Glasgow to Haslingden.

There was one very slight disappointment: I was all agog to see the deeds for the history of this old house, but, alas, it had formed part of the large Wilton Estate in north Manchester and all I received was a brief extract. However, I applied myself to the libraries of Haslingden and Accrington, and with the able and willing assistance of the librarians I made the following discoveries. The initials R.D. stood for Richard Dearden (to this day you can find Deardengate in the shopping area). He had been sent by Elizabeth I to supervise the felling of oak trees. At that time, had you been able to look from a high enough vantage point, your eye would have taken in Rossendale Forest (which can be seen on Ordnance Survey maps), Accrington Forest, and Trawden Forest. The whole of this hilly area was covered with oak trees. Today you will have to hunt for a single one. It was the denuding of the area of its trees that one hundred years later made it possible for the many rivulets that formed to be used in the cotton industry, which needed copious quantities of water. The rivulets were dammed to form reservoirs known locally as lodges, and the lodges supplied the mills with water.

The oak trees, of course, were being used almost entirely for the construction of men-of-war, and the logs were chained together in groups of three. A team of horses then pulled the logs over the ground to the shipbuilding yards. This normally took fourteen days, but races were run—or rather, the teams were timed. The fastest ever recorded was ten and a half days. Great trouble was caused to the inhabitants of the forest because, of course, the squires who owned the land had serfs who relied on the work provided by the squires, and on the forest for hogs, boars, deer, et cetera. All these disappeared with the trees.

To return to Tap Stone House, however, it seems reasonable to assume that it was so called because of the spring in the forecourt, tapped by a well. The records show that Mrs. Dearden committed suicide by drowning herself in the well. Nevertheless, the record also states that she was buried in a white shroud in consecrated ground. That testifies to the authority of Richard Dearden, because in those days those who committed suicide were debarred from consecrated ground. One can only conjecture on the reasons for her taking her own life, but just imagine her situation. As the wife of a government official she must have had some standing in the social life of London. To be exiled to an out of the way area like the Rossendale valley where she would know no one and have no social life at all must have been intolerable. One hundred and fifty years later the descendants of R.D. sold the property and a large area of land with it.

The house became a tavern where the coach horses were changed below the climb to the moors over to Blackburn. It must have been at this time, circa 1750, that the house was enlarged by building, over the well, the room which became my sitting room. The chimney had a "discharge" lintel stone weighing over a ton, and the fireplace was divided into two so that two separate fires and two lots of cooking could go on at the same time. Brackets for the turning spits were in place. Under this room there was now a cellar. The well spring was still running but the well was reduced in depth by about nine feet, i.e., the depth of the cellar itself. The water still bubbled up out of the bottom of the remaining two feet of well and was channeled away to a stone culvert carrying a stream down the hill to the small river in the valley. Stone alcoves for laying wine were built into the surrounding walls of the cellar, and huge hooks for bacon flitches were fastened into the arched roof. The place was shockingly damp until I installed a system of gravity central heating and put a boiler in the cellar.

The property had been taken over in 1899 by the local coal merchant and renovated for the use of the company's foreman, a man named Bentley. His family occupied it till 1916 when the local decorator, named Hoyle, inhabited the house. He was responsible for the excellent decorative order the place was in when I purchased the property. Whenever his workpeople were short of jobs he employed them in the house; hence the panelled walls and ceilings decorated with stucco patterns.

Running My Own Business

While I was getting settled in, Albert was looking for some-where for us to start up in business in Accrington. He found a works in Argyle Street where a retired gentleman had made roller blinds for shop windows. He had made no effort to tidy up after he stopped work, but by shifting his benches, boxes, and sawed-off bits of lignum vitae (the hard wood he used in his trade) to one side, we made an area large enough to work in and rented it at, I think, one pound per week. It was a hovel of a place but had one most valuable asset: the floor level was approximately three feet from the ground and just right for us to walk on to the lorry flat with our four-hundredweight (cwt) fireplaces. We worked in a dump but everything we needed was to hand. Twenty-five pounds' worth of tiles was delivered from one firm, though at least ten had told us we would need to wait two years. Fifty yards down the road was an empty house, the front room of which served as our showroom.

I feel I must observe here that when the devil makes a present it is wrapped around with fancy paper and tied with tinsel, but the inside may well contain a can of worms. When God gives, nothing in its presentation makes it look worthwhile, but inside will be a precious jewel. Surely William Shakespeare had learned this lesson, or how could he have been so perspicacious in his presentation of the case for Portia's hand in marriage to her three suitors. There might well have been, as the Prince of Morocco thought, an argument for choosing the gold casket, but it was in the lead casket that the prize was found, and by Bassanio.

Though my trust in God's leading had, so far as I can recall, never wavered, I confess that the sale of our first fireplace was a wonderful occasion—wonderful that it had been made and advertised and someone had sought us out in that back street.

Wages, sand, cement, tiles, transport, rent, rates, and fitting charges were added up and a profit percentage applied to arrive at a selling price. I think the first few fireplaces were sold for fifteen pounds and, as I say, this included taking out the old kitchen range, building up the gap with good bricks, and supplying and fitting a fireback, grate, and fret front. At this time I was doing a doubly quick changing act: old clothes for the dirty job of mixing concrete, et cetera; clean clothes for interviewing firms' representatives and prospective customers. Albert was driving the lorry and supervising fixing as well as "slabbing." Slabbing is the name given to the operation of laying the tiles down on a solid, smooth table (later on we found old billiards tables were ideal). Timber supported by bricks was used to form the top and sides, and the tiles stuck in place with soft soap. There were different tiles for special positions: flat tiles, round edge or RE, REX for outside corners, and RER for inside corners, for instance. Approximately three cwts of concrete was then bucketed into the basin of tiles and smoothed out to about two inches thickness on the flat and up the walls. Using quick-drying cement called Ciment Fondu, the whole would be set by morning and we could lift the newly made fireplace, clean out the cracks between the tiles, and grout with white cement. In no time at all we had a flow of trade and things were looking very good.

Then we suffered a set-back. During the war the government had allowed the expenditure of ten pounds per year for any new domestic requirement. As this was still in force, the district council refused to give licenses for fireplaces costing more than ten pounds. Since a fireplace was no use unless fitted, that cost was of course considered part of the whole operation. Doing a little trim here, a paring there (particularly off the profit), we thought we could make a go at twelve pounds, but no way could we bring our price down to ten.

However, in addition to the ten-pound annual allowance, two pounds per month could be used for running repairs to a house, so after a considerable battle the authorities finally accepted that two pounds in any one month could be added to the ten, a total of—eureka!—twelve pounds. From then on, for as long as the regulation lasted, we were making austerity fireplaces and fitting them for twelve pounds. We made more profit in the ensuing year than at any other time in the history of the firm. This of course meant income tax, super tax, and the next year surtax on that one year's turnover. Without some sort of illegal subterfuge I do not know to this day how anyone could make a fortune in business.

Nevertheless we were established, and moved into a High Street shop in Accrington. We were expanding rapidly: I found premises in Blackburn that had been used as a garage and repair shop, and Albert took over a small fireplace business in Burnley. The Blackburn premises had very adequate showroom facilities, office accommodation, and a large enough area to take six full-sized billiards tables as a workshop. We were thus able to turn out twelve fireplaces a day, or sixty a week, and the demand for them was sustained. We were now making them with inset shelves, alcoves, and recesses, and selling at between sixteen and twenty pounds according to design and size. Six lorries were in continual use, and newly started firms in the tile trade in the Stoke-on-Trent area were competing for our business. Things were going along swimmingly, but not in every aspect. After almost exactly nine months some fireplaces began to shed tiles, which perforce had to be replaced free of charge, and in one or two instance whole fireplaces had to be replaced.

We found that firms up and down the country were

experiencing the same problems, and no one had an answer. I took out books from the library on cement and concrete making and learned that the major factor was the sand. All sorts of sands were available, but only one was really satisfactory. In our ignorance we had set off by using the most easily available delph sand. Pits only three miles away produced this reddish brown stuff, which made beautiful sandcastles and appeared to be ideal for walling up the insides of fireplaces. It was very easy to use. But delph sand under the microscope was constituted of tiny platelets of molecules; sharp sand, such as washed river sand, was composed of tiny granules roughly cubic in shape. Now if you have ever had two pieces of glass lying flat on each other, you will know that while dry there is no adhesion, but when wet they can only be separated by a sliding action. Thus it is with sand. You can't make sand pies with sharp sand, and to wall up a fireplace required the relatively difficult technique of making sure that needles of cement were sucked into the roughish surface of the back of the tile, thus giving grip to the whole. Delph sand will stand up on its own, but after nine months, when the last vestige of moisture has evaporated, it tends to crumble and tiles held on by atmospheric pressure drop off. No more delph sand, thank you.

Another factor that quickly became evident was that, though Albert and I had to a large extent the same outlook on life, when it came to business we were poles apart. There were several differences. I was dead set against waste, Albert not so much so. We handled money differently, but chiefly Albert was very cautious. I was prepared to take calculated risks, and we got on each other's nerves continuously. Albert found the premises in Accrington, and quite early on we decided amicably to part company. He took Accrington and Burnley, while I took Blackburn and a shop in Sauchiehall Street, Glasgow, splitting everything—tiles, lorries, equipment—right down the middle. I was now my own boss and well content.

Trade flowed easily and further expansion was called for. How wonderful that just when needed, premises on the other side of our west wall became available for renting. All we had to do was make a doorway from our workshop into the spacious area which was capable of accommodating up to 250 fireplaces with room still for four lorries. A large doorway opened onto the street—Merchant Street, to be precise—which led onto Ainsworth Street. At round about the same time another section of the block came empty on our north wall, which provided much needed space for storage of tiles. By now there was a demand for many different colours and shades, and as the war years receded these became available.

In 1952 I was invited to join the Council of the Oxford Committee for Famine Relief, later to be known as Oxfam, and for the next twenty-five years I rarely missed taking the journey to Oxford to attend either the council meeting or, once a month, the executive committee meeting. It gave me a satisfying feeling that I was not spending all my life's hours trying to make money. One was at least doing something to ease the lot of those more unfortunate than oneself, though it seemed more often than not that one could only scratch the surface, making no real progress to alleviate suffering in the world. Looking back, it is obvious that the opposite was true. There is much more suffering today. That one felt better inside for at least making some effort can easily be construed as a selfish motive, but so indeed can the wish to go to heaven rather than be consigned to hell. If you get down to basics, everything one does or tries to do can imply a selfish motive. There were times when I was glad that always with this thought came another. I would imagine myself caught by an earthquake or a flood or civil war in which I found myself and my family destitute, cold, and hungry. How grateful I would be for the handout of a tent or blanket. I went on with my efforts to raise money for refugees and soon found myself chairman of the Blackburn Refugee Aid committee. 1956, if I remember rightly, was Refugee Aid Year, in which a determined and successful attempt was made by Britain and other nations to solve once and for all the problem of the war's refugees and get them rehabilitated.

The following year my business suffered slightly because, although my employees carried on competently during my frequent absences on behalf of refugees, it was I who was responsible for forward planning, and this was somewhat neglected for twelve months.

1957 and 1958, from a worldly point of view, were my peak years. I thought so at the time, and looking back confirms that view—but, as I say, from a worldly viewpoint. I was invited to join the Rotary, I was president of the Blackburn Chamber of Trade, and I was in charge of the Shadsworth Estate Baptist Church, an offshoot of Leamington Road Baptist Church, where I was a member. Business was still flourishing; we were having regular holidays on the Continent and elsewhere. This was before packaged holidays and we arranged our own itineraries. True, there were a lot of what are now known as catch-22 problems in business. There always are situations arising between customers, employees, suppliers, and money where conflicting interests and loyalties vie with one another. I often went to bed at night wondering how on earth a solution could be found to this or that situation. Almost invariably I would refer the matter to the Lord to ask for His help. In the morning it was delightful how things sorted themselves out.

It was obvious that sooner or later all the old cast-iron fireplaces, the removal of which had been the backbone of demand, would be replaced and demand would begin to fall. I estimate that my firm replaced over thirty thousand in twenty years. Fireplaces are not what one would call consumable materials; nevertheless, I told myself that in about fifteen years, wear and tear and changing fashion would necessitate another round of replacement.

That analysis was correct, but the result was not as I supposed. The government decreed that domestic heating should go smokeless and offered large grants to householders to help them change their smoky coal fires into those that would burn smokeless fuel. This gave a temporary fillip to the solid fuel industry in general and my own business in particular. Gradually, however, it became clear that the real boost had been given to the gas industry, which in any case had just had the huge bonanza of North Sea natural gas. Gas fires and wood surrounds began to replace tile. Marble, rough cut marble in small pieces, slate, and reconstituted stone tried hard to compete for a while, but it was a losing battle, for another factor insinuated itself into the scene, viz. small bore central heating.

Whereas in the past central heating had been a matter of using one-inch, two-inch, three-inch, even six-inch cast-iron pipes from a boiler installed at the lowest point of the system, the new system employed half-inch copper pipe. This was a breakthrough, for whereas the old system relied on hot water rising—hence the boiler at the lowest point, a principle known as "gravity feed"—the new method used a pump. No longer did it matter that pipes had to be large enough, no longer did it matter that gravity was relied on to make the water circulate. The pump did it very successfully. Obviously my firm had to diversify and fall into line if we were to stay in business. I found myself very often with the help of my wife having a quick tea and working on to eight or nine o'clock in the evening.

The reason for this was mainly because this was when people were at home. Advice was needed by them, systems had to be planned and materials estimated to give a cost for the job. The size of the radiators to be fitted depended on a strict procedure of measurements to assess heat losses so as to provide adequate heat replacement. The whole scenario had changed. Tile fireplaces were still used, but my slabbing department had dwindled to two workers. The firm was now buying from other firms stoves, surrounds, and pipe that we couldn't make, so that our profit margin was greatly reduced while the constraints and responsibilities increased. Our workpeople had never been in unions, although I had willingly conformed as an employer to the directives from the building unions. These were chiefly concerned with wages, since the conditions of labour in my firm were far better than in the building industry as a whole. Plumbers, however, did belong to the union. In January the building industry decided wage rises, which my chaps automatically got. But then the plumbers objected to the "differential" having been upset, i.e., there was an agreed extra paid to plumbers on account of the additional training they had experienced, and they demanded the same rise as the "brickies" to restore the differential. In June the plumbers' union decreed the rise the plumbers were to get, and of course did receive. The bricklayers then objected that the differential was again upset. For three years, therefore, I paid out two rises in order to keep the peace. But competition was getting tougher, and I personally was working twelve hours a day on a treadmill, struggling to keep the wheels turning and very often having to correct other people's mistakes.

Being in business for oneself began to take on a darker hue, as day after day I found myself at the end of twenty-two years wondering whether this treadmill existence was all I had been born for and all I could expect out of life. Not a happy thought as I recalled the very deep desire I had to run my own business, and how it had been given to me. Meantime I was still going regularly to Oxfam committee meetings once a month and had met C. Jackson-Cole, the honorary secretary of Oxfam and a founding member. We had become quite friendly. He invested £250 in my firm, which, may I remind you, was the equivalent of over £2,500 today. Jackson-Cole was a philanthropist who did all he could to stay out of the limelight. How many people know that Help the Aged was his brainchild? He worked and gave unstintingly to build Help the Aged into the national charity it is today. I could get quite annoyed if I let myself when I think of the many, many people who never give or give reluctantly because, they say, "So much is wasted on administration." That emphatically did not apply either to Oxfam or Help the Aged. Oxfam by now had over two hundred employees, but all of them were inspired by altruistic motives of wanting to do something to help others. Very many of Oxfam's employees had left jobs in the rat race to work with Oxfam at something like two-thirds the commercial salary. Perhaps it was not altogether surprising that I was beginning to think along the same lines. Not that I wanted to be paid by Oxfam. After twenty years on the committee I had no thought of that. In any case I found it enormously difficult even to contemplate giving up my business, even though I had begun to think of it more as a millstone round my neck. It scared me just to think of letting down my employees, my customers, and the many relationships I had built up.

I found myself very humbly beseeching God again to find some way out of this dilemma. I should explain here that my wife had been just as involved as myself in the firm, as its accountant. She had performed her duties in an altogether admirable fashion, taking a wage only half what it merited. Thus she was a boon to the business and a fiscal factor in the family. But one daughter was now married and the other was building a career for herself with the BBC. There was no one who wished to carry on the business. Another quite serious matter was Winifred developing chronic bronchitis. Our family doctor and friend urged us to pack up and go south to a drier area. Three years previously the Blackburn Town Council had declared my premises to be ripe for development and had proceeded accordingly. Tenants in the area were given first choice of premises in the redeveloped area, and I was now in very grand showrooms and offices, but at six times the previous rent. The rates had still to be assessed and fixed. When three years' rates was demanded in the same ratio as the rent, I knew I had received the signal to finish and notified my accountants accordingly.

The National Coal Board, on whose Lancashire Sales Promotion Committee I was chairman, had made tentative suggestions that it might buy my business to use as a sales and advice bureau. Unfortunately for me, all the indications were that the use of solid fuel for domestic purposes was very much on the decline. I was at liberty to sell gas and oil fired appliances, but that was impracticable for the N.C.B. In the end a receiver was appointed who left me to sell the business piecemeal. This was very sensible, for in two or three months I was able to dispose of all but £250 at normal market prices. It gave time for my employees to find other jobs, which they all did, and eventually my wife and I turned the key in the lock for the last time, without the least regrets.

When Jackson-Cole learned of the turn of events and that I was seeking to live in the south, he said, "Good. Come and help me." This included helping him, on one occasion, get dressed in a hurry and rush to Heathrow Airport; re-organising the management of an hotel in Hastings; and fundraising for Help the Aged in Bath and Bracknell. My wife and I spent our weekends for over six months touring London streets in bottom gear. We were seeking new premises for the charity.

My remit was to find property at a rent of not more than one pound per square foot that was large enough to accommodate all departments of Help the Aged with a little extra for expansion. A difficult factor was that it had to be near tube stations so as not to incommode the staff more than necessary. I found a number of premises, which were turned down by Jackson-Cole and/or his committee, before I found Denman

Street, Piccadilly. I shall always consider that they missed a real "snip," probably by being over-cautious.

Cleveland House came up for sale during this period. It was served by Metropolitan, Circle, and Central lines at Marylebone and Baker Street stations, only a stone's throw away. It consisted of four floors and a basement. The ground floor and first floor were empty; the second and third floors were occupied on short-term leases. The asking price was £110,000, and I arranged for a mortgage with Legal & General Assurance. The annual cost for this was approximately £11,000, the whole of it being assured by the rents from the two top floors. The committee turned it down. Twelve months later the premises were valued at £250,000, and two years later when the top floors came vacant Help the Aged had expanded and desperately needed the extra space. Heavens above!

Something Other Than Mere Chance Governs Our Lives

Jackson-Cole did not like his Christian name, Cecil, and no one ever used it. Some of his contemporaries in his earlier days called him "Jacko," but that only applied to a small coterie of admirers. I could never use it and solved the problem by using his initials. He was C.J. to me all through our twenty-five years of association. He and I had many discussions on religious matters but never made much progress. He seemed totally to have accepted a thought expressed by Sir Gilbert Murray (the founder of Oxfam) that "God is continuously seeking to right the wrong done by evil people." All his life C.J. exerted his energies in doing just that. His secretary opined that he was building up credits in heaven. He did a great deal for Toc H (an association concerned with the spiritual needs of soldiers); he spent a great deal on promoting and supporting the Churches Council for Health and Healing, and had me promote a committee in Manchester under the chairmanship of the bishop of Middleton. I acted as secretary. It petered out after three years. He supported the faith healer Dorothy Kerin and took me along on one occasion to visit Burrswood. This hospital at Groomsbridge, near Tunbridge Wells, is a fine old mansion standing in 230 acres of delightful grounds. It is a registered charity, administered by a board of trustees, and provides a perfect place for sick people, the terminally ill, or for convalescence. Dorothy Kerin, its founder, was miraculously cured herself and had the gift of faith healing.

That was a project before my time but it was quite obvious

from the reception he got when we arrived that C.J. had played a part in acquiring Burrswood. Jackson-Cole died at Burrswood on 9 August 1979. When his first wife, Phyllis, died he had created the Phyllis Trust in her memory and through it financed the charity known as Voluntary Christian Service.

Indeed it was this latter function that first made me sit up and take notice of this extraordinary man. Shortly after I had joined the Oxford Committee for Famine Relief (Sir Gilbert Murray had already passed on), Jackson-Cole was, as I have previously stated, the honorary secretary, and he was advocating using more publicity to attract funds. He startled me by suddenly standing up and saying, "If the committee will consider more fund-raising events, I will make a contribution of thirty thousand pounds." (I must remind my readers that that represents more than three hundred thousand pounds today.) I was astounded; it was quite some time later that I learned he was offering to fund the operation from the funds of the Voluntary Christian Service. Very little came direct out of his own pocket. He always contrived to pay out of some source or other rather than in his own name. The only time of which I am aware that he paid out directly was at the A.G.M. of Help the Aged in its early years. Annual General Meetings are not known for large attendances, and he overcame this reluctance by *giving* a dinner. That certainly got people there, but he was careful to state on the agenda that the dinner had been paid for by an anonymous donor.

To me C.J.'s view of God was very inadequate, but I never got him to alter his view. I seldom expect to change anybody's ideas by talk. Part of the reason for *being* is that we learn by our own experience, which may of course sometimes reinforce what a person has heard from others. The verbal aspect will be quite overshadowed by the fact of the experience. When I was studying electrical engineering I learned that if you passed an electric current through wire coils wound round a bar of metal, the bar of metal became a strong magnet. It is only a powerful magnet while the current is flowing. Pull the switch and the magnetic field is largely lost, but not entirely. There is left what is known as residual magnetism, about 5 percent of the full power, and this is more or less permanent. Years ago I magnetised a screwdriver this way, and it is still very useful for holding onto small steel screws.

I find life itself has a similar aspect. Each experience we suffer or enjoy appears to us as a vital and sometimes traumatic part of life. When it has passed there is only a residual effect, but it is this residual effect that is permanent and influences all our thought and action subconsciously for the rest of our lives. It is a vital part of the law of cause and effect, which states that every effect is the cause of something else and every cause has its effect. I would ask you seriously to consider the following proposition. If this law has been operative from the very beginning of human experience, and if each individual experiences every day at least fifty examples of the working of the law, and this applies to an average of one thousand million people every day for the past, say, six thousand years, is it surprising that the mind cannot comprehend how complicated the day-to-day manifestations of the working of the law have become?

Every single thing that happens is the result of a long string of results brought about by every effect having a cause and being itself the cause of another effect. So we use certain words to try to explain the situation, chief of which is the word *chance*. Others are *coincidence, accident,* and *luck*. There is no such thing as luck. Luck is the inevitable result of many, many instances of cause and effect too involved for anyone even to begin to work out. You may not agree with me, but you cannot argue against it because you know no more about it than I do. It is a matter of belief.

Most people think that accidents happen in split seconds

of time. That is no more true than is the notion that the condition of a vehicle's brakes or steering, or the driver's aberration, is the cause of a car accident. The results are frequently too traumatic for such trivial factors to be the *cause*. They are undoubtedly contributory factors but are not in themselves the cause. I have myself on more than one occasion missed seeing an approaching vehicle at a corner, or not observed the person standing on the curb waiting to cross the road, or been guilty—though not often—of excessive speed, and *escaped* being involved in an accident. I maintain that more people have had the experience of near misses than they have of serious results. This must be taken into account when considering accidents and the many more occasions when accidents are not the dire result. We must look elsewhere for the reason why some lose arms or legs or even suffer death. These effects are far too serious to be the result of a moment's aberration. If that were the case, life would indeed be unjust, but then life itself cannot be condemned, because life is the sum total of our experience in *being*. Life itself is neither just nor unjust; we must look elsewhere before we can point the finger of blame, and I shall not be able to get to that point in the next few pages. It is involved, but let us stay with motor accidents and particularly one that involves two or more cars. How did two cars come to be at the same spot at the same time and collide? The drivers had probably set out at different times from points at different distances. They had travelled at different speeds, been stopped by other traffic a different number of times, and had different personal requirements involving stops. The list is as long as the journey itself, and yet they had arrived at exactly the same time and tried to occupy the same spot. Some years ago I recall seeing a play on television that succinctly illustrated what I am saying. What happens to cars happens to trains and airplanes, et cetera. A multitude of miscellaneous events of cause and effect go into a mishap.

It is probably true to say that any misadventure begins to evolve hours, days, even weeks before the climax is observable. Who was it said, "I am the master of my fate, the captain of my soul"? I challenge that. It could possibly be that we are each of us captains of our souls, but we are not thereby masters of our fate. There are far too many other factors outside our control. How many times have you been told that "so-and-so would have been on that train, plane, or ship but for . . . "? All of us have had occasions when we have been saved from certain events by inexplicable occurrences. That is to say, inexplicable to us. By the way, the converse is just as true: that we have sometimes been involved by circumstances outside our control, viz. fog on a motorway, for instance.

No matter how many laws are passed to make travel safer whatever the mode, no matter what precautions we may take ourselves, there is always an unseen power which can and does override. Do you say that is fatalism? Not at all. I am building up my argument towards its later conclusion, which to me says that worldly thinking has gone wildly awry.

Watch a game of snooker and it is often a matter of simple observation that one man is going to lose. You see him making mistakes that at another time he would avoid. It happens to tennis players, to golfers, even to football and cricket teams. That unseen force is thwarting their best endeavours, or alternatively aiding the other party. People don't generally pay much attention, they merely say so-and-so was unlucky and forget about it as something outside their own orbit. They are right: it doesn't concern them unless they have a deep desire to learn the truth of the nature of such phenomena. When I was in my teens my fiancée and I played contract bridge against my parents on Saturday nights. What thoroughly enjoyable evenings they were, always with a little cigarette smoke and a lot of good humour floating about. We were well matched, which fact I think contributed to my ultimate conclusions. I suppose the permutations on how the cards fell are enormous, yet after two or three years it dawned on me that there was a pattern.

I am sorry that I cannot give precise examples of what I mean. It is sixty years ago, but I became convinced that chance alone was not the motive power. There was rhythm to the play, which seemed to say that someone or something was controlling the fall of the cards and often enjoyed playing jokes on the participants. After my experience with the Ouija board I now partly believe that guides, demons, sprites, poltergeists—call them what you will—enjoyed our Saturday evenings as much as, if not more than, we did. One could say with fair certainty that once or twice a month one would find oneself with five or six spades or any other suit. As regularly as clockwork the time would come round for one to hold enough honour cards to call a grand slam. Once in ten years, which is to say in about three thousand games, I found myself holding a full suit of hearts. The temptation to call seven no trumps was great, only to find myself without a single trick, because I could not get in to play my suit.

I am treating this subject lightly because I have not studied it sufficiently to see how playing cards is affected by the law of cause and effect. Nor have I attempted to investigate further how, if at all, spirit powers might influence the way cards fall. I have, however, turned away from games of chance, from lotteries and prize draws. I have never entered a raffle, and Bingo I know nothing about.

Earning is more important than receiving, and to receive what has not been earned is altogether objectionable. (A present from a friend is not included because it has been paid for.) I cannot of course conceive of any way in which I could win a prize draw because I don't indulge in them, but if I did get a sum of money in this way I should be horrified and sick. That is my own view for myself; I do not suggest it as a course for others except for one vital point. Everything has to be paid for, and, morality apart, when you receive what you have not earned a price will be exacted some way, somehow.

People talk of the law of averages. What is the law of averages? The very term itself suggests that things happen in such an orderly fashion that they balance out. Ecologists have come to see that nature itself on this basis proceeds in an orderly fashion.

So what of *chance*?

I have listened enthralled to David Attenborough. He does a splendid job but, oh, how I wish I could spend an hour or so with him on the matter of chance. He believes that chance brought everything about; chance and natural selection brought us into being, and chance, to him, must still be operating. But chance, by definition, acts vaguely and unpredictably, otherwise it isn't chance. David Attenborough has said that quite by chance things happened in the past that added up to the producing of fish, reptiles, birds, and animals, but his use of the word presupposes that life proceeded in an orderly fashion. Nowhere along the line did chance undo what had already been done. Chambers defines chance as "that which causes things to fall out or happen fortuitously or without assignable cause." This is not what I understand by *chance*. *Fortuitously* suggests a benign influence, and the use of the word *assignable* leaves us with the word *cause*, merely suggesting that mankind has not yet had the wit or lived long enough to find the true cause. Well, that at any rate rules out God, and of course David Attenborough is a self-confessed agnostic. The alternative is that chance itself is God. But if chance means, as I contend, that the totally unpredictable can happen at any time, then chance has the power at any time to return us to the primordial chaos from which it is supposed to have rescued us and all things. I much prefer my own idea of God as knowing where He is going and how He is going to get there, i.e., a God with a purpose.

But let us stay for a short while longer on evolution by natural selection. As I understand Darwin, he never suggested, as some say, that a potato could become a carrot or a dog could become a horse; the line for each started much earlier, but there is the "rub." No one has been able to define the start of any given species. Granted such situations spread over aeons of time, but it is poor argument for the supporters of "the origin of species," every time they come to something they cannot explain, to fall back on the lame excuse, "Oh, it took millions of years." What a wretchedly empty explanation it is when faced with a somewhat different type of living creature to say that "chance built up power like an electrical condenser, and then took a leap forward." True enough, once started, arms, legs, wings, tails, and eyes have evolved and improved, but how did they start? What are the origins of the eye? Then again, if evolution is so powerful, how is it that so many creatures seem not to have evolved even over hundreds of millions of years? The crocodile, for instance, and the coelcanth. With what glee was the discovery of this ancient fish made and publicised. Why had it not evolved into something different? I think these people destroy their own arguments.

What force of evolution first caused an "eye" to be produced? Granted, sight has evolved in different ways according to the specific requirements of "natural selection," but what started this process? What stops growth? Why do plants, trees, creatures stop growing? Surely the concept of an idea must come before the fact. What power of evolution provides that concept? The answer of course is Intelligence. And that presupposes Divine Intelligence. Given that, there are no further problems to evolution by natural selection because there is a controlling influence at all stages. I am open to correction, but the general law is that all elements expand on heating and contract on cooling. Yet water disobeys this rule and, fortunately for life, suddenly at four degrees Celsius reverses the process of contraction and begins to expand into ice. Think what would happen if it did not. Divine Intelligence decreed that it should.

But to go back to chance. If chance rules our lives then it must rule the world, and if it rules the world it must therefore rule the universe. How can anyone hold such a preposterous notion? If unpredictable chance ruled the stars, what mayhem could it cause? Instead we see perfect and tranquil order. Order so precise, so sure, that astronomers can calculate to a split second such phenomena as eclipses of the sun and moon, the return to view of Halley's comet, and many others about which I confess I know nothing.

It is much, much easier and far more satisfying when contemplating the glory of a sunrise and looking in my diary to find that on April 20 it rose at 4:56 and set at 7:05, whereas on April 27 it rose at 4:41 and set at 7:18, it is far more satisfying, I say, to believe that there is *intelligence* behind it all. I have found many people who would subscribe to that view. George Bernard Shaw did. I have not found a true atheist in my life. The difficulty for most folk comes in trying to see that Divine Intelligence as a Personal God, that is a Creator so powerful as He must be, yet who can take a particular interest in me and you and everyone else. You remember me telling you about my period of unemployment. What a fantastic risk I took! As I said, I had nothing, I saw nothing that would suggest that my God had even heard my prayer, let alone was willing and able to answer it. Yet it was so, and He proved to me that long before I was aware of it He had taken steps to fulfil my deepest desires. How glad I am that I found the strength to trust. Yet faced with a different set of circumstances it is still a test of faith to "wait upon the Lord." Every new dawn can only be born out of darkness; every new joy can only be born out of trial and suffering.

I *know* that God *is* and He knows me.

The BBC's Blue Peter Christmas Appeal 1969–70

Earlier I intimated that I had done some fund-raising for Help the Aged in Bath. A section of the charity concerned itself entirely in building blocks of flats for the elderly, supervised by a warden. A site in Bath had been chosen and building was progressing. I reckon Bath to be about the most interesting, most beautiful city in England, but its inhabitants are not the "hail fellow, well met" type. I enjoyed the city, its Abbey, its river, its buildings, and its environment, but I have never felt I succeeded very well. When I organised a sponsored walk the rain poured down so relentlessly that only thirty-one walkers turned up. The next time I insured against the weather, and a quarter of the proceeds was taken to pay the premium. Jackson-Cole was keen on me organising a dinner and inviting well-to-do people to it, with of course the idea of getting them all to stump up. Lord Strathcone and Mount Royal, who lives in Bath but whose ancestral home is Colonsay, just south of Mull, was very helpful and agreed for me to use his name on the invitations. Naturally certain of the HTA (Help the Aged) staff were invited and, apart from the noble Lord, were the only ones that accepted. The dinner was cancelled. I have learned a lot since then. Such functions can appear to be very successful, but it is the preceding groundwork that makes them so.

Then there was the utter failure of my most notable success. It was my wife's inspiration to contact the Marquis of Bath, who at the time had a lion that people could approach.

The idea was that the lion should be on show, sitting in the chair of a weighing machine, and people would file past, tossing coins into the pan, until, hopefully, the scales tilted. What a hope! There was no way we could have collected coins to equal five cwts of lion. However, the Marquis, while being very willing to assist the project, said he thought Monarch was getting too old and a bit crotchety. Instead he offered to sit in the chair himself with a lion cub on his lap. Very sporting! So I obtained permission to use the Abbey Court, an area bigger than a football pitch, and arranged an awning, carpet, bunting, and large Help the Aged banners. I got all the schools to join in with collections beforehand and publicised the occasion well in the local press. This was about six weeks prior, and I set about finding a chair-type weighing machine. There used to be any number in places like the Golden Mile at Blackpool, where the stall holder would guess your weight. You only paid if he was more than two or three pounds out. You generally paid. Were any of these about in 1969? Definitely not. Avery Scales, the manufacturers of weighing machines, had their representatives searching the country for me. The whole show depended on that machine, but not one could be found until the last weekend. And where was it? In a storeroom at Bath race course. It was one hundred years old and had been used to weigh the jockeys until spring balances took over. I was most thankful that they agreed to loan it to me.

So the day arrived. I had organised a one-way traffic flow, but what happened? The whole of Bath tried to get into the Abbey Court. It was so congested that only the first arrivals got near the Marquis and his lion cub. In desperation I sent people out with collecting boxes, but they could hardly move. The expenses for the occasion were £101 and I collected £102.

Well, it wasn't a financial success, but when I first went to Bath no one knew about Help the Aged and its flats for the elderly. After this Saturday no one was unaware, and help started to flow. Furthermore, this Bath episode led directly to the next effort. Again I want to credit my wife with the inspiration to contact the BBC and, more particularly, the children's programme "Blue Peter," thinking that they would be interested in the Marquis of Bath and his lion cub. It turned out that they had just recently made a programme on Longleat and were not thinking of another. (Longleat is the ancestral home of the Marquis of Bath and is situated a few miles outside the city. The grounds are extensive and now include an animal safari park, hence the lions.)

However, I was certainly doing the right thing at the right time, because the programme had involved itself in what was then well known as the Blue Peter Christmas Appeal. For six years this had been on behalf of some needy project abroad, and Ed Barnes, the producer, had begun to think that, perhaps, they should now consider help to some British project. The idea of helping the aged in this country particularly appealed to him and his staff. He said that if I got in touch with him again in September when they would be considering the December appeal, and if I could satisfy him on four points, there was a good chance that they would be interested. The four points were:

1. Propose something in which children could be specifically involved.
2. Propose an aim that would lend itself to an attractive programme on television.
3. Find a warehouse large enough and convenient enough to accommodate the masses of parcels that would flood in.
4. Have a big enough voluntary staff to deal with un-wrapping and disposing of the useful article designated in item 1.

Quite an undertaking it seems as I write it down now, but I was brim full of enthusiasm. Item 1 had to be a throwaway article with no value on its own but worth something in a mass. It had to be something that children could easily obtain without harassment to parents, and which could be despatched easily. If I say it was fortuitous that at that time the nation was changing over from an assortment of two-amp, five-amp, and fifteen-amp round pin electrical plugs to the now-conventional flat pin 13 amp, I am not thinking of the dictionary definition of chance. I saw it and still see it as the Divine Intelligence giving me a helping hand. Don't forget that years previously He had found me a house, the money to pay for it, and a job all in one week. Brass was then worth £360 per ton, which made it a worthwhile proposition. But we made another suggestion that made Ed Barnes positively excited. What about the children sending in broken Dinky toys and miniature cars? "Just the thing," said Mr. Barnes. "It will involve the kids in giving their own possessions." Zinc spelter was worth £65 per ton.

Item 2 gave us more trouble. Help the Aged, and C.J. in particular, wanted help for the flat-building programme, but baths, sinks, and toilets were not considered suitably photogenic on a T.V. programme, and the producer wanted something "that would move." Another department of the charity was creating day centres for the elderly, and they required facilities to transport them. The "Blue Peter Old People's Bus" was just the thing. Specially designed with safety-belted seating, hand rails, a low step, and a lift-type platform, the Rootes Group was able to provide such a vehicle at about twelve hundred pounds each. This was ideal, as it would be seen by children on the streets as the result of their efforts.

Item 3 was solved by the kind assistance of the Greater London Council, which of course was in existence in those days. They had a four-storey warehouse in Stewart Street, number 57, which they were prepared to let me have at the "peppercorn" rent of £250 per month. (In the event we used the premises for five months for £250.) It had ground floor, basement, and three other floors, and for most of that time the whole of it was in use. I had of course to pay for getting the lighting, ceiling gas heaters (well out of the way of all the paper), and the lift to function. The latter was most essential. At peak flow fifteen delivery vans a day were coming from the post office, and two whole floors were full of unopened mail bags holding about one hundred parcels each. The basement was choc-a-bloc with wastepaper. On Christmas Day 1969 the appeal had only been going a fortnight and an area on the ground floor, thirty feet long by ten feet wide and ten feet from floor to ceiling, was stuffed full of parcels waiting for attention.

Item 4: organise a voluntary force of workers to handle the parcels. Obviously to pay staff to do this job would defeat the object. I contacted over forty youth clubs in the Greater London Area and almost without exception they agreed to send approximately thirty people on a given night. No group would need to come more than twice, or so I thought. To have someone on hand every night of the week except Sundays needed careful arranging, but well before the starting date I had a rota.

In addition, of course, I needed to dispose of the sorted metal. Two local "rag" firms were most helpful in providing transport, and one gave a large quantity of reinforced manila bags capable of holding sixty pounds of metal. A firm in Stevenage accepted the regular deliveries and melted down the toys to form ingots of zinc spelter. The brass was much more valuable but much less in quantity.

One thing worked in our favour: to save postage, the children (or their parents) broke up the unwanted plugs and sent only the brass, so we were not unduly troubled with the Bakelite bodies. Two things I had not allowed for, however,

61

slowed up the work considerably. One was the way in which the children had pushed brass pins, et cetera, into the bodies of the zinc cars. They simply *had* to be extricated. The other was the fastidious way in which the children had wrapped up their precious gifts. How I cursed cellotape!

The volunteers were, to say the least, enthusiastic. Their exuberance was difficult to control. When I opened the doors for the first time I had no idea of the many facets of the operation that were going to enlarge my own education!

From the word go, we had of course mixed boys and girls who sat together at the tables provided and talked as they worked. Practically the only subject of conversation was SEX, with no holds barred and no taboos. I had never contemplated hearing such open conversation in my life. I only vaguely had knowledge of the words used to describe the anatomy and actions. Any idea of instilling my more Puritan attitude to sex was out of the question. Had I succeeded I am sure they would simply have packed up and left. I gave up and got used to it.

I provided each worker with a large bag for wastepaper. Again, it was useless. In half an hour we were knee-deep in wastepaper on the floor. This had to be gathered up afterwards and kept temporarily in emptied post office bags in the basement. Deliveries to a wastepaper firm were made weekly. Not much was obtained in cash for this, because the paper was very mixed and little of it was of good quality. But it was all grist, as also were the stamps, which we had removed and sold by weight, with the exception of Channel Island denominations, which had a value in their own right and of which I myself still have a full set, though I do not collect stamps.

Quite a number of people sent in brass articles, which were sold separately for far more than scrap value. I still cherish an old bell I purchased and even the Chinese brass vase of 1423. Date and dynasty were moulded into the base. Alas, it turned out to be a Birmingham-made replica.

As I have said, the number of parcels was large. Neverthe-less, I was surprised at the number that turned up that should not have. Mostly they were Christmas presents, and of course as soon as we realised the situation a system of checks was devised and these parcels were kept for return to the post office.

Not all was thus returned! Indeed, the first intimation I had was from a small group of local children who, to my initial surprise, came every night. I was beginning to have a great deal of trouble with parcels torn open and left in the pile, and it was only when I caught a couple of these local lads lying snugly in the dark amongst the unopened mail bags upstairs, drinking whisky they had found, that I began to realise the implications. The interest of the locals was solely in the unexpected bonanza of Christmas presents. Naturally I stopped them from coming in, and that was the cause of a whole lot more trouble.

In the meantime, however, the "Blue Peter" team—Valerie Singleton, John Noakes, and Peter Purvis—were making regular visits, and videos were made of the operation for the television screen. On one occasion they brought their own team, organised from Saint Paul's School. That was a very successful and relatively quiet evening.

They all entered into the spirit of the thing, but of course never forgot that they were the BBC or its representatives. Valerie Singleton was always rather aloof, Peter Purvis was a relatively new boy at that time, but John Noakes was one for whom I took an instant liking. He would very much have liked to buy my little bell. Pictures were taken of the mail vans arriving, the bags being unloaded, parcels being opened and sorted, and finally the deliveries to the smelting works in Stevenage—lorry loads each week.

I had long had a wish to see what a *million* of anything amounted to. Since we collected a million and a half toy Dinky cars, I now have a good notion. On average we filled ten or twelve sixty-pound bags a night for over two months. Sad to say, very shortly after the New Year, when the appeal no longer appeared on the "Blue Peter" programme, which had handsomely achieved its object of not one but five Blue Peter Old People's Buses, the interest of the youth club volunteers waned and I was frantically trying to bolster up my rota. The WRNS, WRAFS, WVS, YMCA, YWCA, and many other organizations were approached and generally lent a hand willingly. I am sure that the spirit of co-operation is stronger in Britain than anywhere else in the world. It was not sufficient. I had a little team of four or five seconded to me from the Help the Aged staff, but they had little time for sorting after shifting bags and paper, loading, et cetera. By the middle of March, HTA were becoming desirous of seeing the job wound up. "Blue Pete" had gone on to other things, and the post office was getting restive about the many mail bags I still held. Parcels of course had stopped coming in, but we had a backlog of two storeys of mail bags at the end of February.

And then I had a brainwave! What about getting prisoners to do the work? When I tackled the home office they were as stuffy about the idea as one might expect from bureaucracy. But the governor of Pentonville welcomed the notion. He immediately saw the potential interest for his inmates. So I hired a van, and twice a week my little team loaded 350 mail bags and delivered them to the prison. There a gang of men was ready and quickly shifted the bags inside. At the next visit, there were the toy cars and brass all neatly sorted and rebagged. The prisoners thoroughly enjoyed the change from routine and greatly appreciated doing something worthwhile. They all knew about the programme. So in three weeks we had cleared up and finished. I still find it curious that though the governor of Holloway was keen, the women were totally uninterested and would not co-operate. The women on the whole were much more aggressive than the men.

The Blue Peter Appeal revealed several aspects of life

previously unknown to me. I have mentioned the sex talk, and I have intimated that shutting out the local youth caused trouble. It was a good thing that 57 Stewart Street had corrugated iron sheets fastened to cover all windows before we went in, because now, every night, there was a fusillade of missiles thrown at them. One night when we left the premises we found a hundredweight of rotting cucumbers in front of the door. Remember that the wholesale fruit and vegetable market of Spittalfields was just across the road down the street. Several of our helpers were mobbed, but only one lad to my knowledge was seriously injured—and he was one of the locals. He had shown a much more mature attitude than the rest, and I had encouraged him. Indeed, I'd told him that I would get him a permanent job if he wanted it. One night the gang attacked with broken bottles and he was slashed in the back. I had to rush him to hospital in my car to have a dozen stitches. We called the police on more than one occasion, but they said they could do nothing unless we got hold of the ringleader.

Opposite the market and on the other side of the street at right angles to Stewart Street was a piece of open ground fenced in with a high wire fence. This was where at four o'clock to six o'clock the produce lorries used to arrive and unload their goods onto trucks belonging to stall holders in the market. It was a favourite spot for the meths drinkers. About twenty of them permanently inhabited the area, existing on methylated spirits (which sometimes had been treated by bubbling gas through a rubber tube), on stolen fruit and vegetables from the market, and by a fire stoked by wooden crates and rubbish from Spittalfields. The meths drinkers went to the nearby men's hostel at one shilling (five pence) a night, if they had the money. Otherwise they slept by the fire. On Christmas Eve two of them had kipped down in the gateway to the unloading area and covered themselves with paper. A lorry driver, supposing what he saw was a pile of rubbish, ran over the two men, killing one and seriously injuring the other. On more than one occasion the fire brigade came and doused the fire and the refuse collectors cleared up the mess. To what purpose? As soon as they had gone the fire was started up again.

It was on this corner that the gang of youths met. One particularly rough night made me determined to do something about it; so the following evening, during a lull in the uproar on the shuttered windows, I asked for volunteers. My plan was to execute a lightning raid on the gang and grab someone. I only got one volunteer. We quietly opened the door on the side street, rushed across, grabbed one boy whom I knew to be largely responsible, and ran back to the door. It was done so quickly that the rest had no time to take in what was happening and react. We were fortunate. My next act, of course, was to contact the police, and in half an hour a whole contingent arrived complete with a senior officer. The lad, usually all bravado, crumpled and was taken away. I believe that the police did no more than extract names and addresses and went to each home to warn the parents of the likelihood of severe action if the rowdyism didn't stop. It most surely did stop, and I even got help from two more boys. From Andy I got no help. Andy was a lad of nine, well known to the police, who said they had no authority to take action till he was ten. The action would be to see he attended school, because he played truant every day. His mother went out to work and his father, a long distance driver, was away all week. Andy was simply left to fend for himself and was quite capable of doing so. He smoked continuously and rarely went home before four o'clock in the morning. He was attracted to us by the free cups of coffee and biscuits, but he was not by any means dependent on this. He disappeared one day, and the lad who had his back injured said to me, "He's off to the market for his lunch; he will come back with his pockets stuffed with fruit." So it was. Andy never needed any money; he never paid for anything. Woolworth's supplied all his needs, gratis and for nothing. Indeed his mother used him on similar errands for herself, and he always helped himself to cigarettes for them both. He was small and looked like a cherub—a cherub who used dreadfully bad language. I have said that we were well barricaded at windows and doors, but there was a small semi-circle of glass about ten inches deep and ten inches across above the main door. One day I arrived to find this glass broken. Andy had squirmed through the opening and ransacked the parcels for presents. There was such a mess that I doubt he could have done it all by himself. I could not see how he could have let anyone else in, though, because the doors were all padlocked.

Our final operation was an auction at Phillips. This was the first of several in later years organised by or on behalf of "Blue Peter." It came about because shortly after Christmas one or two men came in the evenings, asking if they could go through the bags of toys for collectible items. It was not long before it became a routine operation for each full bag to be emptied onto the concrete floor and five or six businessmen, dressed for the office, to go on their hands and knees, sorting through the pile for special types. This certainly had its humorous side, especially as one man kept on his bowler hat. I take it for granted that in their own peculiar way they profited by the operation, but they found and put on one side a considerable quantity of little cars, buses, et cetera, which subsequent events proved them to be right in saving. Finally the amassed assortment was analysed and categorised. Phillips Auctioneers catalogued and advertised the auction and the whole affair was shown on the "Blue Peter" programme with John Noakes at one time acting as auctioneer. People came from far and wide at considerable expense. They spent liberally, some a couple of hundred pounds. I learned that one or two men had even purloined the family holiday savings and spent the lot. The whole business was a whimsical affair, but it raised

Blue Peter Old People's Bus auction of collectable items of toy cars. The author is at the far left, John Noakes, far right.

£760, i.e., the equivalent of over ten tons of spelter, and added a new dimension to the Blue Peter Appeal.

The total raised was £12,500 and purchased five Old People's Buses, plus bathroom equipment, electrically operated chairs (delivered to Northern Ireland), and an assortment of aids for the elderly. The simplest and probably the most effective of these was a padded cushion doubled in half with a strong spring on the hinge; thus, half of the cushion rested on a seat while the other half was raised at approximately forty-five degrees. This folded flat when sat upon, but with slight pressure from the person on the arms of the chair it gave instant and effective lift to the body. The cushion was simple but most welcome to elderly people whose legs were beginning to fail. It should be remembered once again that at today's values each of the buses would cost the equivalent of the whole amount raised, so the sum we raised equalled approximately £140,000 at current values. It was a truly worthwhile exercise.

Self-discipline Needed in Sex

The incessant and lurid talk about sex at the working tables was not the only aspect that assaulted my sensibilities while in the London area. The public conveniences were places to avoid if possible. Some very peculiar things happened there, generally only recognisable by a quick, furtive action on the part of the couple of men who were there when one entered. On one occasion I actually caught a man in the act of hoisting up his trousers. Generally such toilets were in quiet places, but the underground convenience in Leicester Square was a hotbed of illicit action. Then there were the suggestive advertisements on the escalators in the tubes, and the much more blatant publicity in Soho.

There is nothing like this sort of thing in the provinces, thank goodness, but there is still too much on the radio and television programmes. I deliberately watched (it took some effort) a programme called "Scarfe on Sex" just recently. Despite protestations to the contrary it was designed to titillate; no doubt about it. If adverts and such programmes have not that effect, as some maintain, what other reason is there for them? For over twenty years I have supported the National Viewer and Listener Association and am glad I have done so. It has at least acted as a brake and prevented the runaway trend witnessed in other countries. Mary Whitehouse has suffered much vilification, but I believe she has done a noble service to this country. What has surprised me beyond measure has been the small amount of support from the churches. In a church of three hundred members I could find no more than half a dozen who were interested in the association's efforts. "Couldn't be bothered" seemed to typify the attitude of most people, but some, like a doctor friend of mine, were antagonistic. The doctor took the view that, left alone, the sex issue would "burn itself out." I find it a most interesting proposition. My friend Albert told me once that he had read an account of how Buddhist monks were subjected to having to watch nude women until they were totally disaffected. It may well be true that men who indulge themselves to the limit eventually tire of the excitement, but there are others who will just be starting on that road and who perpetuate the exploitation of sex. Is there then no end while human beings exist?

In the meantime there is a growing list of very dubious but legalised activities with genes, with artificial insemination, in vitro fertilisation, et cetera. These activities are more and more taken for granted.

There opens up the wide expanse of the consideration of evil in all its many forms. There is no exact dividing line between good and evil, at least none that at present is discernable by the human mind. Rather is the situation like the seashore, the very place where, according to Darwin and others, life itself first emerged. The area between high and low tides is an area of fluctuating, alternating experiences forcing change. In like manner evil touches us, wets our toes and sometimes washes over us, and the soul or spirit of each one of us is being throughout life subjected to these variations in very similar manner to the original plasma of natural life. This is again another factor that I propose to consider with others in my final chapter. Interaction is a key word.

For the moment I want to propound a theory that I admit is idealistic in the extreme, but that in itself commends it to the thinking person. Many people are and for many years have been concerned with population growth, striving with might and main to preserve life but having as yet little success in "family planning." Many years ago I was responsible for moving a resolution in the executive committee of Oxfam that we should support family planning—as the lesser of two evils, i.e., the use of contraceptives to control birth (which is unnatural) on the one hand, and the population explosion and its attendant dangers on the other. It was passed with a large majority, though not unanimous. I personally had grave misgivings, which have not receded over the years. About the same time I attended one of those rare meetings in Rotary that was open to both sexes. It was addressed by women and the discussion was on family control and the use of various contraceptives. All the discussion was on how to have intercourse without *risking* a birth, and for over an hour all the comments and suggestions put the whole responsibility on the woman. At last I could stand it no longer and jumped up to say that there were two involved in a partnership but I had heard nothing at all about what the man should or should not be doing.

It was taken for granted that the man's desires must somehow be satisfied. That is the general consensus of opinion. The woman must protect herself as best she can. It is indeed men, their appetite, nay, their lust, which creates big families and which is responsible for the population explosion. But to suggest that men should control themselves, as I did at this meeting, is totally ridiculed. Heavens above, why?

At this moment millions of people are living in arid areas, on swampy ground subject to devastating floods, on the sides of volcanoes, and in earthquake land, largely because they have nowhere else to go.

The Bible says, "be fruitful and multiply," but it also forbids intercourse immediately before, during, and after the menstrual period to prevent the new birth from being adversely affected by impurities in the blood. This results in there being a "safe period" of approximately seven to ten days when the uterus is withdrawn. It is rare, but not impossible, for conception to take place at this time. If men had from the start observed such a restriction and been prepared to abide by it, i.e., to exercise personal control on themselves, not only would children have been much more free from disease but population increase would have been under control from the start.

One of the reasons given for large families, especially today in the East, is that it safeguards against high child mortality and ensures support for the parents in old age. The more abstemious approach would have had the same effect because children would not have died at such alarming rates. The Levitical laws, you might say, have not been seen by everyone, but they are only an extension of earlier existing rules and taboos in human society that are practised and adhered to very satisfactorily amongst the so-called primitive cultures from Papua, New Guinea, to the American Indians to this day.

I say again what I said to start with, that this idealistic approach never had a chance in practice and today no doubt will be considered morally unattainable, but it would have enormously reduced death rates and suffering in many other ways.

Doubtless God in His omniscience would know this. How much more desirable is such a small effort at self-control than all the agonising about this or that method of preventing conception by unnatural means, not to mention the agony of abortions.

Why does God allow it? This is a question often asked, and my final chapter gives the answer. For the moment suffice it to say men and women have brought it all on themselves, and the foregoing paragraphs on sex are a very clear example of how and why.

My Trip to America

Shortly after the Blue Peter Appeal for Help the Aged, I was asked to go to America for Oxfam, to evaluate and report on the practicability of fundraising there by the normal methods of Oxfam U.K. at the grass-roots level. By this is meant shops, coffee mornings, bring-and-buy sales, sponsored walks, small concerts, i.e., raising money in relatively small amounts but by many people and at frequent intervals.

The Americans, who had formed an autonomous committee, tended to think large: big donations from wealthy people, large concerts, and of course their best-loved scheme of regular mailings of "begging letters." Not everyone in Britain will know that lists of people interested in anything under the sun have been compiled and are available for sale. Who, for instance, is keen on violin music, buying melons in case lots, reading, gardening, flying kites? You are able to purchase a list. Obviously people not only make a good living out of selling such lists but there is considerable demand in America. Personally, to get begging letters four times a year I find irritating even though it might be a cause I wish to support.

When I visited the schools to see if I could arrange sponsored walks or swims I was received cordially but negatively. It was the general belief that the scholars would join in the effort willingly but I would never see the proceeds. Everyone was most willing to listen and talk. The director of Dumbarton Oaks, Senator Taft, and Dr. Harris at the University of Charlottesville were all very agreeable. Dr. Harris had just broken his leg and was confined to bed, but he sent his daughter thirty kilometres to pick me up and give me dinner at his home. Talk was easy, but getting something actually started was more difficult. The American committee itself must take most of the blame for this, of course, because anything I conceived and organised had to come through it. Sadly, it didn't. Following my success with "Blue Peter" I was extremely desirous of getting a recycling programme going in the U.S.A. Conditions were ideal; the idea was a talking point with the general public, and Reynold's Metals in Richmond was en-thusiastic. Remembering the difficulties of unwrapping and disposing of the paper, I suggested that it would be adequate simply to tie two or three aluminum cans together with a label attached. Reynold's of course had its own furnaces for smelting and agreed that there was no objection to the label and string going in with the tins. The firm was prepared to stand the cost of publicising the scheme because it was "just what we want." The whole scheme was organised and ready to start before I left the States, but it never got going. I must say I was very disappointed. It would have raised thousands of dollars.

Needless to say, I found some time for sightseeing and visited the homes of Washington, Jefferson, and General Lee. Amongst other things I visited the Capitol, the Smithsonian Museum, and the grand memorial to Lincoln. I was also present on a special day at the Cenotaph. Two years previously, Con-gress had decreed that nothing else be allowed to be higher than the Cenotaph, and this included kites. I was in Washington on the Saturday that this ban was removed and witnessed the joyful resumption of the flying of kites around the memorial. I did not get inside the White House, but I shall always be grateful that it was the reason for blocking what would have been a minor catastrophe.

I was preparing to take a photograph of the White House when a nearby tourist asked me to help him decide the speed and aperture for his picture. My own camera had a built-in exposure meter, which I prepared to use to help him, but I knew from practical experience that it was not giving me the right answer. On checking, I realised that the setting for the speed of film had been changed. Just before leaving for the States, my camera had been to the makers for repair to the shutter, and in testing the firm had used a film much slower than I was used to, and altered my camera accordingly. But for this incident I could have taken every shot in the U.S.A. at the wrong exposure. As it was, only the photos I had taken from the plane were ruined. That was bad enough, however, because the captain, to avoid head-on winds, had flown the northerly route from Prestwick, which took us over the south of Greenland. For three hours all that could be seen below the plane was cloud, but as we approached Greenland the cloud cover broke and for ten minutes we had the most spectacular view of the mighty black peaks of the south coast, with their snowfields and glaciers reaching down to the frozen edge of the sea. The ice sheet on the sea finally dissolved into the blue Atlantic. It was an impressive sight, and my photographs were hopelessly over-exposed. Fifteen years later, again head winds caused the plane I was in to fly the northerly route over a blanket of cloud, which broke for ten minutes over Greenland, and once again through this hole in the clouds I was able to photograph that wonderful land, this time making very sure of the correct exposure. That mountains and valleys, snowfields and glaciers can still be so impressive when viewed from thirty-two thousand feet says something for the grandeur of the terrain.

The world would call that coincidence, which is a word frequently used for circumstances not properly understood. I think there are much more precise and benign reasons. It pleases me to think that by divine power I was given a second opportunity to enjoy that sight. If we are obedient to the divine rules of living there is *nothing* impossible in this universe, just as the Lord Himself stated in Matthew, chapter 21, verse 21. As these words make clear, faith is of the essence.

> Verily, I say unto you, if ye have faith and doubt not, ye shall not only do this that is done to the fig tree, but also, if ye shall say unto this mountain, Be thou removed, and be thou cast into the sea, it shall be done.

Another very deep and important point is brought to the forefront. It is evident to me that my disappointment in the first instance had sunk deep into my subconscious and had clearly become a prayer—a prayer that I did not know was there until it was so delightfully granted. Now, this *is* prayer, which happens to and in all of us. We all have these submerged yearnings, which God grants *in His own time*. This is prayer, and quite different in character from the mind's copious production of pious expressions, which are no more than wishful thinking. This is a subject in itself and I must come back to it later.

To return to America. At the end of my stay I flew out to Des Moines for a few days. I achieved nothing, unless, unknown to me, in later years my address to a sorority brought fruit. It was an experience in itself to gaze over the endless acres of corn in Ohio and realise that only one hundred years previously they had been interminable miles of flat prairie to be covered by the wagon trails. It was also intriguing that a week earlier it had been cold enough in Washington for it to snow. Here in Des Moines it was about ninety degrees Fahrenheit.

I returned to Britain from Des Moines via Chicago and New York. Approaching Prestwick, I had a glorious view of the Hebrides in the evening sunlight.

C. Jackson-Cole died on 9 August 1979 at the Burrswood Hospital at Groomsbridge, near Tunbridge Wells. A memorial service was held in St. Martins-in-the-Fields. At the same time I ceased to take an active part in both Help the Aged and in Oxfam, though I still support both charities. The Oxfam Committee in America is today very active and successful using its own methods of fundraising.

Some Salutary Lessons of Life

1978 was the year that I learned about hospitals and surgical operations. Up till then I had nothing worse than a bad cold and had little to do with doctors. For a couple of years at least I had suffered from osteoarthritis in my left hip, and in May 1978, after much heart searching and prayer, I had the operation. My experience of the efficacy of faith healing had led me to expect this trouble somehow to be dealt with in the same way, but it was not to be. Overall—left hip in May, prostatectomy in June, infection of the bladder in July, and right hip operation in December—I spent seven weeks in the hospital and enjoyed almost every minute. No responsibilities, just lying or sitting, looked after like a baby. About all I did for myself was clean my teeth. The open ward for me was much more acceptable than the dull drab silence of a private room. The food, except for one meal, was always acceptable; I positively looked forward to the deliciously fresh crisp salads of Sundays. The one exception was the overdone toasted cheese on toast. Someone had been too zealous with the grill.

When it came to a surgical shave, I had mixed feelings, especially when, without lathering, the barber brought out of his kit an outsize old-fashioned "cut throat" razor. He powdered my hairy abdomen liberally and with great sweeping movements removed swathes of hair like a farmer mowing hay with scythe. My alarm at possibly losing a vital part was unfounded, however, as he expertly manoeuvred his blade round delicate areas and I was left smooth as a . . .

For some reason that I have never fathomed, I found myself

much more emotional than normal. Often a thought or a phrase in a book would bring tears to my eyes, which was quite abnormal for me. I read the whole of Josephus in hospital, despite the difficulty of finding a convenient way to rest the considerable weight of such a large tome, especially after having one's tummy cut open to remove the prostate gland. I shouldn't be surprised, by the way, if my gland was the last one ever taken out; the scraping method of removing excess tissue was already well advanced.

Josephus was the Jewish army commander at the sacking of Jerusalem, circa A.D. 74, and the Diaspora, who later became chief historian for the Romans. The most significant thing I have to report, however, concerns what happened after my first hip had been done. Two days later the surgeon and his team were at my bedside and quite casually remarked that I had been given the normal two pints of blood. That was a shock to me! It took me back abruptly to 1937. As chief accountant of the Glasgow Depot of Exide it was part of my duties to liaise with the doctor on his monthly visit to check on the health of the men handling lead acid batteries. Dr. McPhail gave me, a newly married man, a lot of new and useful information on marital relations, some of which I have already mentioned, such as the frequency of intercourse. Blood transfusion was then becoming widely accepted and blood donors were being sought. Dr. McPhail brought a form for me to fill in, which I duly did. When it came to my signature I found I just could not sign. My hand with pen hovered over the spot and I was unable to put my name down. Until the moment I have related when the doctor told me I had had a transfusion I had never regretted not signing. But to have benefitted by a transfusion from someone else when I had refrained from participating myself, I recognised immediately, was all wrong, and I was shocked.

That the body benefits enormously from blood trans-fusions is unassailable; it saves it from the trauma of loss of blood and plasma and enables it to recover much more quickly than otherwise. The argument against it is, of course, Biblical. In Leviticus there are severe strictures against ingesting the blood of animals, hence, the Jews eat only kosher meat. If it is wrong, dangerous, and inadvisable to eat blood, because of the impurities that it carries, how much more inadvisable is it actually to transfuse blood direct into the system.

Not many will agree with me, and I confess I am unable myself to be firm about it, as you will see. It is the old antagonism of flesh over spirit. Those that support transfusion can be and are objective in their argument; those who favour the spirit can only be subjective. Being subjective does not carry much weight with the modern technology of today. Nevertheless, I am about to relate what happened when I was faced with the operation on my right hip. I am perfectly frank and sincere; I could not make up my mind whether to agree to the transfusion or to say I did not want it. As I say, I recognise the efficacy of blood transfusion on the immediate result, against which a spiritual objection appears feeble, despite the now-known dangers of contracting AIDS, which certainly points the moral.

AIDS was not a problem in 1978, so I did not have that particular information with which to make a decision. I struggled with the problem even as they wheeled me into the operating theatre and finally could only confess to God my inadequacy and make a little prayer, albeit a sincere prayer: "Lord, I cannot decide, do Thou undertake for me." Two days after my operation, when I was taking an interest in things around me again, the surgeon and his staff came to see me. His first words were, "You are a curiosity." "Oh," said I, "why?" "Well," he said, "we had two pints of blood ready for transfusion and we didn't use a drop; you didn't bleed!"

To be in business for oneself, you may or may not have confidence in God. It is certain that you need more than the usual quota of self-confidence. My pride has already been mentioned, indicating that I had my full share of self-confidence—to the discomfort, often, of those with whom I came into contact. From 1979 on I had not the same worldly need for such self-conceit, and I am sure I am right in saying that with the hip operations God was taking me in hand to reduce and finally remove that pride. Almost like Jacob, whose thigh was put out of joint (Gen. 32:25) and for the same reason, I found myself free from pain but with a limp. At the age of seventy this does not significantly interfere with physical activities; indeed, on my seventieth birthday I gratified a long-standing wish to climb Ben Nevis, not quite reaching the top in thick cloud and rain because I hadn't allowed myself enough time to get down again before night. The reason for the limp, of course, is that it serves as a continual reminder that I am a creature of flesh and blood, and God's desire for me, as for everyone, is the perfecting of the spirit. All the infirmities of old age are designed to encourage the soul to relinquish its hold on the body and prepare for the real life to come.

If it were not for my sure belief that God knows what He is doing, I would feel sad that so many do not seem to realise this fact, or if they do, do not accept it. So many doubt that there is a life hereafter. And all the time the life here is only a preparation for the life to come. The Lord told Nicodemus that "ye must be born again, and become as a little child." That is, we cannot enter the Kingdom of Heaven unless we are sufficiently humble. Any depreciation of physical capacity is more than worthwhile if it helps us towards this end. It is not that to become as a little child is the passport into heaven, but that childlike trust *is* heaven. It is only by becoming like Christ that we can see Christ.

He was "obedient unto death, even the death on the cross." We must become obedient to Him. All the experience of life is God teaching us this Truth, for Christ is the life, the truth, and the way. As the Lord Himself said, "Wherefore if thy hand or thy foot offend thee, cut them off and cast them from thee; it is better for thee to enter into life halt or maimed, rather than having two hands or two feet to be cast into everlasting fire." Strong stuff, and I am convinced that churchgoers as a whole do not pay much attention to it, believing as they do that it represents an element of hyperbole in Christ's teaching. That would be to accuse Christ of sinning, for does He not say "But let your communication be, Yea, yea; Nay, nay; for whatsoever is more than these, cometh of evil" (Matt. 5:37).

Hip replacements, arthritis, impairment of hearing and of sight—if we trust God these things will be accepted cheerfully as necessary constraints for the betterment of our souls. They should be regarded as God's pruning of the vine's branches. These thoughts are totally in line with the earlier comments on the real reason for accidents. God sees and knows everything that goes on concerning us; even the sparrow does not fall unnoticed to the ground, and the very hairs of our head are all numbered.

Prayer—Real and Imaginary

The foregoing thoughts, from the answer to my prayer re transfusion to the realisation of the absolute need for true humility, form the appropriate backdrop to a deep consideration of the all-important subject of prayer. But let me here quote Juliana of Norwich, that pious, hermit-like abbess of the sixteenth century.

> Though we be highly lifted up into contemplation by the special gift of our Lord, yet is it needful to us therewith to have knowing and sight of our sin and our feebleness. For without this knowing we cannot have true meekness and without that we cannot be truly blessed.

Outside the Bible itself there has never been made a more illuminating and profound statement than that. Contemplation of it takes one to the very threshold of the kingdom of God. Sin—the merest wisp of a thought that deviates from the perfection of God is sin. A rich man came to Jesus and said, "Good Master, what good thing shall I do, that I may have eternal life?" And Jesus immediately rebuked him, saying, "Why callest thou me good, there is none good, but one, that is God" (Matt. 19:17).

I have had my moments of exaltation by the grace of the Lord and immediately afterwards said, done, or thought something that I knew was wrong. At such times one does indeed "hate" oneself. Repentance must follow before forgiveness can be sought, and it is a bitter pill when you know how many times you have had to ask for forgiveness. It seems impossible that you can ever reach holiness and maintain it. "With man, it is impossible," said Jesus, "but with God all things are possible."

How upside down it seems that to come anywhere near the kingdom of God we not only have to have knowing of our sin but have withall to suffer the humiliation of learning that we cannot be truly humble without that knowledge. "Oh, Lord, how great are thy works, and thy thoughts are very deep" (Psalm 92:5). We have to know that in the moment of our utter weakness, when we are totally dependent on God and His mercy, when in the extremity of our surrender, then, and then only, can we enter the Kingdom of Heaven.

All the trials and temptations of the spirit, all the humiliations of the flesh, and all the pains and problems of being human, have meaning; all are designed in mercy and love by the supreme will of God to bring us to this point. A place impossible for us without the grace of our Lord, Jesus Christ!

For sixty-five years or therabouts I have known a German song:

Es ist im leben hätzlich eingerichtet, das bei dem Rosen gleich die Dornen stehn, und was das arme hertz auch sehnt und dichtet, zum schlusse, kommt das voneinandergehen. . . .

A sad little song because it points a truth: that with the rose comes also the thorn, and what the poor heart craves comes with an unwanted circumstance. A sad song because it rightly states a truism but does not suggest a reason or moral, which is that we are not intended in this life to find perfect conditions. We are not meant to find anything so delectable that we seek to keep it.

We are two beings in one, soul and spirit, body of flesh; and as Paul says, "the carnal mind is enmity against God" (Rom. 8:7). I suggest that the whole of this great chapter be read earnestly. No words of mine can state the situation better. The body is the soul's training ground to fit it for the life to come.

All this must be appreciated fully before one can come into the right condition for prayer. The aspirations of the soul must be separated from the flesh. The mind itself can conceive the most wonderful phrases, and does so with ease, but they are not necessarily prayer. Often what we hear from the pulpit is 49 percent minisermon (the speaker talking to us rather than to God) and 49 percent wishful thinking. Such wishful thinking when carefully analysed is actually insulting to the Creator. It tells Him in effect that He is making a mess of things and that if we were in charge we should do things very differently. Of course the reason for this is that we subconsciously think that the evils we pray to have changed are the result of some other power in the world that God is striving (and failing) to correct. Remember Cecil Jackson-Cole? That was his conception of the situation exactly. Yet in the next breath we are declaring that God is omnipotent. How inconsistent! But mankind is inconsistent; he doesn't stop to think out what he is saying. How else could the Germans in the last war pray for victory while at the same time people in this country were praying to the *same* God for victory for themselves. While Saddam Hussein exhorts Allah to grant him victory, the archbishop of Canterbury is praying to God for a successful outcome to the Gulf War. If men and women would stop to think seriously of such inconsistency (which they certainly acknowledge exists), they might come to the correct understanding that neither approach represents true prayer. It is all wishful thinking of the mind and does not in any way reflect what the soul of man should be contemplating with relation to God and His mighty purposes. How can it, if the soul itself doubts whether in fact God Himself is operative or whether it is this other power interfering?

How often we think thoughts of our own and represent them as God's thoughts. Why? Because we are wrapped up in the proud belief that we can in our strength make supplication to God. The ego in each of us does this repeatedly and then, to make sure that we are on the right lines, pops in the phrase "All this we ask in the name of Jesus Christ." Sunday after Sunday and weekdays in between this phrase is used like an incantation that is going to effect what we are after. Well, of course the mind, and thus the tongue, can easily produce the right sounds, but where is the heart and soul in all this?

We must *know* the will of God before we can use the expression "in His name." But do we? I submit that we never allow ourselves time to consider what is the will of God. To begin with, most would say that we cannot know the will of God. Then how can we say "in His name"? This phrase presupposes that we know and understand the will of God.

If the boss of the firm goes to an employee and says, "Here is a message I want you to deliver to so-and-so," that man will go and deliver the message in the boss's name and not in his own. So if we speak "in the Lord's name," we must *know* that it is He who is commanding. If we are not sure on this point we cannot possibly do or ask anything "in His name."

Furthermore, if we are really acting in the name of the Lord, it would not be necessary to say so—it would be evident; otherwise the expression is without value and has indeed become meaningless in the context of practically all so-called prayer, whether on Sundays or any other days.

How do we then stand in relation to reading prayers from a book or a leaflet? They may be couched in the most beautiful language, but if they are not our own they will be secondhand *unless* we are concentrating to the point when they become the expression of our own heart and soul.

The hymn writer, James Montgomery (1771–1854), put it succinctly in his hymn, the first verse of which starts,

Prayer is the soul's sincere desire
Uttered or unexpressed
The motion of a hidden fire
That trembles in the breast.

Yes, there you have it. But most people sing the hymn without paying attention to what they are saying. Indeed, is it not everywhere acknowledged that the Lord's Prayer is more often than not repeated parrot fashion without any real concentration on the words? It is quite possible to take the words of others and make them your own, but I suspect that this must be very rare.

Prayer is not the ephemeral expression of pious thoughts. These may have their place in worship; they are so well accepted that they are taken for granted, but they must not be understood as prayer. An acceptance of this statement gives the answer to the so-called "problem of unanswered prayer." There is no such thing. God answers all prayers, but not everything that is offered by men and women is prayer.

There is, in fact, only one prayer: "Thy Will be done." But two others, I believe, are acceptable to God: the plea "Lord, have mercy upon me, a sinner" and a heartfelt prayer of intercession that offers a sacrifice. Thus Moses, praying for the forgiveness of the Israelites when they had been caught worshipping the golden calf, asked God to forgive them and added, "but if not, blot me, I pray thee, out of thy Book of Life."

These three convey the all essential elements of humility and obedience. Against this, the vast ocean of verbosity that pretends to be prayer is of little avail.

Finally on this subject, what of the unconscious prayer? It is demonstrable that many people, believers and nonbelievers, make prayers of which they are not conscious until, that is, they are answered by the all-seeing, all-knowing Creator of men and women, for He knows their innermost desires. I know that in my life there have been quite a number of occasions when I have only realised that I have been praying after God has taken action on my behalf.

While I was unemployed and waiting on God to set me up in business there were very many occasions of what, to me, was earnest prayer, but I believe, too, that God Himself was aware of very deep prayers of which I personally was not conscious.

Now I come again to my opening paragraphs. My wife had died on 7 November 1980, and I was unable to think of anything in the Bible that covered the situation so effectively that I could find complete peace of mind and heart in it. While, of course, I had moments of deeply felt emotion and tears, I had abundant trust in the Lord Christ and accepted the will of God with equanimity; nevertheless, there were a number of questions that I dwelt on as often as possible and for as long as possible. Incidentally, why tears? They flowed unbidden at a thought or word in a way that could hardly happen now. But what was the situation? I kept asking myself.

On the subject of death, Jesus three times referred to it as sleep. Lazarus, He said, slept. Since we are unconscious in sleep of the passage of time, I could well believe that all people that died slept peacefully until the Resurrection morn. To them it would not seem that any time at all had passed. It would be to them as instantaneous as if they had indeed passed straight from one sphere to another. Paul says, "Behold, I show you a mystery; We shall not all sleep, but we shall be changed. In a moment, in the twinkling of an eye, at the last trump; for the trumpet shall sound and the dead shall be raised incorruptible, and we shall all be changed" (I Cor. 15:51–52). Jesus promised the malefactor, "This day, shalt thou be with me, in paradise."

Again we have to remember another curious expression of the Lord's, which for years was to me quite inexplicable: "And another of His disciples said unto Him, Lord, suffer me first to go and bury my father. But Jesus said unto him, Follow me; and let the dead bury their dead" (Matt. 8:21–22). Light came, as I believe, by inspiration of the Holy Spirit, when I realised that the Lord was saying "let the dead [in spirit] bury the [carnal] dead." Always we have this distinction of the life of the spirit, the soul, and the life of the body.

So I contemplated these portions of scripture as well as the story of that other Lazarus, a beggar who lay at the gate of a rich man and who, when he died, was carried by an angel into Abraham's bosom while the rich man, when he died, suffered the torments of hell (Luke 16:19–31). Neither of them was asleep in the sense that he did not know what was going on. And again Jesus reminded the Sadducees firmly that "I am the God of Abraham and the God of Isaac, and the God of Jacob; God is not the God of the dead but of the living" (Matt. 22:32). The problem at that time was to me as complex as had been years earlier the problem of conscientious objection and what could or could not be done in wartime. The answer to that had been simple in the end.

And now my Gracious Lord did something for me that I shall forever treasure. I realise that some will pooh-pooh what I am going to relate, some will be very sceptical, but to me it was golden.

My wife died on a Thursday and on the Tuesday following I was alone in my home and stood at the kitchen sink, I think peeling potatoes for dinner. I became aware of something over my left shoulder and behind me. It came and went again. Then it came more strongly and receded once more. The third time it came fully—please don't scoff, it is sacred to me—a vision of my wife's face surrounded by what, for lack of a better description, appeared to me as a four-inch halo of pink candy floss. My wife was full of health and vitality and was smiling broadly. The vision had shoulders but no arms, and the shoulders were deep pink. It was like a cloak of pink light grading to white at its base. It was lovely to behold and is more fresh in my mind now than my daughter, whom I see every day. But it was the words Winifred spoke that assured me that this was no figment of my imagination; they were so exactly appropriate. She said, "This is something you never expected, isn't it?" Indeed it was, and now any thought of my wife at any time is accompanied by this glowing vision, which lasted, perhaps, four seconds, and I know without a shadow of a doubt that Winifred is not sleeping but is very much alive and happy. Thanks be to my Lord, Jesus Christ, for His wonderful compassion.

It was evident then and remains surely still that the vision was an answer to a deep, deep prayer of which I was not actually conscious while meditating on the various scriptures. In the same way it appears to me that the intent with which I concentrated on the problems of conscientious objection for six weeks in prison constituted prayer. Seemingly it is not necessary to address your thoughts to Almighty God for Him to know what is in your heart. He sees.

And again one's attention is forcefully drawn to appreciate the difference between prayer on this level and the mere use of a string of words issuing from the mouth. I believe that this deep prayer is not by any means the prerogative of believers. At certain times in life it is concomitant with strongly emotional occasions for practically everybody whether they believe in God or not. Even atheists will have to acknowledge that they have life and where there is life there is the Creator. It isn't necessary always for us to have cognisance of our inner state; God knows. A number of people have spoken to me of their experiences of answers to prayer of which they were not aware until after the event. There are innumerable stories of people in adventures and mishaps by land, sea, and air, in which they have acknowledged help from an unseen source. I have one particularly happy event to relate in my next chapter.

Blue Lagoons, Coral Reefs, and Palm Trees

In all the years following the war the family had many delightful holidays together, always touring and often on the Continent. When the children had grown up and were "doing their own thing," my wife and I went still further afield to Turkey, Tunis, and Morocco. I suppose that it is a common human trait to picture in the mind places that one intends to see for the first time, and I should say that invariably the place in reality never came up to expectation. One exception to me was Marrakesh in Morocco. Never could my mind have conjured up the glowing, warm, and exciting city that I discovered when I finally arrived there, but the whole of that holiday was picturesque and adventurous. When, therefore, I found myself living alone after my wife's death, holidays seemed to have lost their appeal. Visiting new places is an experience one can savour best with a companion to share it with. Visiting well-remembered areas on one's own seemed to me to be pointless.

Four years passed without my discovering any interest in foreign travel, until the day that a High Society Travel Agency brochure fell through my letter box. It offered five or six packaged holidays to the South Seas. Now, if there was one area in the whole world that I would have liked to visit, it was encapsulated by any island in the Pacific Ocean. As a boy I had thrilled to read *Treasure Island, Coral Island,* and of course *Robinson Crusoe.* Not having the slightest opportunity to go to such places in my youth, the desire had been pushed into the inner recesses of my being and forgotten. Forgotten, that is, for sixty-five years, till reawakened by that brochure. I found myself planning a holiday of at least a month for when I should have sold my home and had money to spare. I planned to sail out on a passenger-carrying freighter and fly back. At one time you could get a ship from half a dozen ports in Britain that would take you anywhere in the world. Not in the 1980s you couldn't. Only one British Line from London went to Singapore, and that wouldn't take anyone over sixty-five years of age because they did not carry medical facilities to cover all requirements. The Gdinia Line from Poland could be boarded at Hamburg and seemed to offer the basis of a plan, but only three months after contacting the company I got a letter to say that it had discontinued the voyage. I had in mind a trip when I should be about seventy-eight or seventy-nine years old, but the Lord God had a different idea. He knew better than I that while at seventy-three I had still plenty of energy, the situation was going to be much less favourable in another five years. God, and God alone, set in motion the sequence of events in 1983.

Whenever a new idea is given to me from two different sources, within a matter of days I know that the Lord is speaking to me. Thus, when the director of Help the Aged sent me a personal letter suggesting that I should consider augmenting my state pension (the only income I had) by taking out an annuity on a portion of the capital in my house, and when a few days later an entirely unsolicited approach was made by Hambro Insurance offering just such a scheme, I had to take notice. The upshot was that I mortgaged twenty-five thousand pounds of the value of my house, but I had nothing whatsoever to pay until the house was sold. It was a mortgage in reverse. By that I mean that the calculations were based on normal building society rules for mortgages, but *I* was the recipient of the income on the supposed loan of twenty-five thousand pounds. Now, eight years later, it was the most advantageous transaction of my life. Of course, it has to be said that had I died within two or three years and my executors had to sell my property to redeem the loan, the overall picture would have been very different. The fact is that I have been receiving a very considerable income for the last eight years, *plus*, and this is the crux of the story, a lump sum of £1750 to do with as I liked. Even with £450, which I knew I could afford, this was still £800 short of the needed figure to send me to the South Seas. But just as I was receiving this lump sum, the government did something that had never been done before, i.e., it offered shares in Post Office Telecommunications, now British Telecom. It wasn't a gamble; it was a rock solid certainty that if I invested the whole of my money I would be able to sell at a profit. I did. I got exactly the £800 I needed for this proposed holiday. I am not the only person to recognise that when God is dealing in money He does so in exact terms. The devil may be a bit above or a bit below the required figure, but it is the hallmark of God's interventions that it is exact. Billy Graham tells a story of how in Portland, Oregon, fifty years ago approximately, he needed a sum of money. People tried to persuade him that he had enough to decide to go ahead, but Mr. Graham said, No, if God is guiding me we need another £1500 (I believe that was the figure), and it was that amount that came in the post the following morning. Another vital indication of God's leading is in timing. He is never a little before and certainly never a bit late. Remember my own experience in being given Tap Stone House by Him.

It is an ever-present human failing that we want time to spare. We want things to happen before they (to us) get desperate, but God decrees exactitude. How is it that astronomers can calculate to exact fractions of a second? How is it that NASA can rely on computerised calculations of journeys and orbits in space? Just stop and think what would happen if God's universe was as haphazard as men would have it.

I now had three thousand pounds and I had a problem. Was it right to spend so much on myself? Ought I not to give it to needy causes? I readily confess that I did not feel enthusiastic about this latter course, and I easily convinced myself that not only had the Lord initiated the move for me to fulfil a lifelong dream but had actually planned it for now rather than in the future. The whole project was unfolding for me, even to a switch to Jet Set Tours, which offered me all the same facilities but allowed me to pick and choose. I chose to spend three days in Fiji but to go on almost immediately to Tonga for six days, thence to Western Samoa for five days and return to Fiji for thirteen days. It was a very full programme and I realised after all arrangements had been made that I could have done with one more day in Fiji and could afford one day less in Tonga. Two weeks before I was due to depart Jet Set phoned me to say that Polynesian Airlines had cancelled the flight that I was booked on from Tonga to Samoa. What a blessing that the tour operators had almost instant communication with the other side of the world by telex. When it was sorted out I went from Samoa to Tonga, lost one day in Tonga and had my extra day in Fiji.

All my life I have experienced an impatience that was disquieting. Always in the car I could only partially enjoy the journey because of my itch to arrive. I could not properly enjoy today for thinking about tomorrow and, oh, if my plans were thwarted by some unforeseen hitch I would be irritated!

That was why, when we were delayed in Turkey in our journey from Antalya to Denizli and driving needlessly fast in the dark (there was absolutely no cause for hurry), I overshot a corner and landed eight feet lower than the road, in a field. For this South Pacific trip I was so certain that the Lord was directing that I determined to take things as they came and to enjoy the present moment whatever it offered. In other words I entrusted every moment to God and knew His peace. This worked so perfectly that I determined to live the rest of my life on the same basis and have known the peace of God ever since. There was one newly discovered factor that contributed hugely to the efficacy of this decision. Isaiah, chapter 45, verse 7, states, "I, the Lord, form the light and create darkness, I make peace and create evil: I, the Lord, do all these things." The implications of this statement are profound and I have devoted my next and last chapter to them.

So, on the morning of 1 September 1985, I rose at 6:00 A.M. The sun was streaming into my bedroom. It was a beautiful morning. My friend and neighbour had offered to take me to Gatwick Airport and we lunched together before setting off at about 4:00 P.M. It was then that I had my second chance to see and photograph Greenland, though we flew over cloud for the whole journey except for ten minutes over the southern tip of this majestic land. Thanks to flying westward, the sun that set at 4:30 A.M. (British summer time) as we were landing at Los Angeles was the same sun, i.e., Thursday, that had greeted me in my bedroom. From L.A. we flew to Hawaii and thence to Nandi airport, Fiji, arriving at just after 4:30 A.M. Fijian time, having crossed the international date line and lost a day. In actuality I was travelling forty-eight hours from leaving my home to arriving by coach at the Naviti Beach Resort on the Coral Coast. I went immediately to bed and slept till dinner time. The hotel spread itself over a large area with almost all bedrooms overlooking the lagoon. The en suite rooms were commodious and air conditioned. This last can be a mixed blessing when it has been *added* to the facilities; you don't know whether to leave the noisy fan on or switch it off and sweat. At the Fijian hotel where I stayed after my Blue Lagoon sail to outlying islands the air conditioning was built-in and silent. However, the Naviti Beach was excellent, free and easy, yet with Fijian happy, courteous service. At this time I stayed only one full day and then was off to Western Samoa, recrossing the date line.

As we took off in the nearly empty little plane (seventy seater) and climbed into the clear blue sky I was so overcome with exultation that tears streamed down my face, because it was at this point I realized what a deep desire to visit these parts had been quietly present in me over all the years since my childhood reading had awakened it.

Not only were the physical elements—the plane, the sea, the sun, the exotic sight of tropical islands in the sun—quite delectable, but the truth that God Himself had known and understood the desire, had purposed to make it possible for me, and had indeed organised the arrangements in detail, this truth, I say, broke upon me like the thunderous rising of the tropical sun.

Here was proof that not only did Almighty God hear and answer prayer as He had done when He set me up in business, but He was obviously aware of, and willing and able to realise, a prayer of which I myself had not been fully aware. Here and now was the evidence in full measure that all the hopes and prayers that one expresses in church services (and only half believes) were known unto God, provided He could see they were from the heart and not just wishful thinking. How do you and I tell the difference? We can't, really; only God knows a person's heart, but we may sometimes have an indication in the intensity of emotional impact. Prayer, I must reiterate, is not the simple expression of words it is so often taken to be. To quote the hymn again:

Prayer is the soul's sincere desire,
Uttered or unexpressed,
The motion of a hidden fire,
That trembles in the breast.

So I had arrived in Western Samoa, an island paradise where today, as one can imagine, there is a considerable mixture of cultures. Ancient Polynesian customs, dwellings, and agriculture interwine by tarmac roads, fine hotels and with all modern transport, almost entirely automobiles of Japanese manufacture.

I was staying at the Tusitala Hotel in Apia and within an hour of my arrival was strolling on the sea-wall above the little harbour before going for my evening meal. There occurred an incident that has been to me like a thorn on a rose bush. I was the thorn. A little girl, about twelve to fourteen years old, wanted me to buy a little homemade fan for two tala (approximately £1.80). Not only was this an outrageous price, but I did not want at that moment to be badgered into buying anything. She quickly dropped the price to one tala, then added a conch shell and finally the few cents she had in her hand. But I was hard-hearted and resisted her until she finally and resignedly turned away. She had hardly lost herself in the crowd round the market-place when I was smitten with remorse. Up till now I had treated her as just another "tout." Now that it was too late, I realised how desperately she wanted to go home with a little cash. How easily and painlessly could I have made a little girl happy. Here was I, spending about fifty pounds a day, and I had missed a wonderful opportunity to be charitable, nay, magnanimous. Now I felt real pain and dashed into the crowd in a vain attempt to find her and make amends. I went out onto the sea-wall every evening hopefully to meet her again. A few people in Samoa and later in Tonga benefitted from my remorse, but to this day the pain of recollection has not been assuaged. How it emphasises human failings—mine anyway.

Needless to say, I saw fruit bats, blow holes in the volcanic lava build-up against the sea, breadfruit trees, poinsettia bushes, frangipani, and lots more before I returned to Fiji and the Naviti Beach Resort, where I stayed several more days before embarking on a short cruise of the Pacific and its many exotic "islands in the sun." The Blue Lagoon cruise was the highlight of this holiday, comprising as it did concerts given by the inhabitants of the various islands, dinner parties on the white sand beaches and among the palm trees or in caves formed in lava flows by the sea's edge, snorkelling in the lagoons, and many other delights. Returning to Fiji, I spent my last four days at the eminently satisfying Fijian Hotel.

It is not my intention to give a day by day account of this holiday, for I am sure that everyone has experienced holidays just as good, but rather have I hoped to show how little say I had in matters from beginning to end, and how much I saw the Hand of a Beneficent Father.

To this end I would like to relate one other instance when I had no doubt about Divine direction. There were two excursions, both of which I was greatly attracted to. One to the so-called Orchid Island near Suva, an area full of Fijian natural history and culture, and a trip up the Manua River to a hillside village deep in the Fijian jungle. As both required a thirty-mile coach trip over much the same ground, and were therefore fairly expensive, I hesitated to indulge myself in both trips and finally chose the Manua River.

In company with half a dozen others I set off. After travelling for over an hour we arrived at Orchid Island, quite a distance from the river. The driver had forgotten to let us off! So I visited the nature reserve and enjoyed it without feeling any of the irritation I would have done previously. This took the whole of the morning and I was advised that I could catch a yellow coach from the Trade Winds Hotel back to Naviti. The hotel provided me with lunch and a sight of the specially constructed platform over the lagoon with its teeming population of tropical fish, but no bus. I was still remarkably unconcerned as the afternoon wore on, just interested to see how things would turn out. About 3:30 P.M. one of the blue Jet Set coaches stopped at the hotel on its way to Suva. It was actually taking employees back home, and one of them recognised me. "What are you doing here?" she said. "You are supposed to be on the Manua River trip." When I explained what had happened she was, of course, most concerned. "You paid for the Manua trip and I'll make immediate arrangements to put you in for tomorrow. Meantime we have to get you back."

She arranged to take me into Suva with them and then to return from Suva to Naviti on a non-stop coach. The following day I went on the river trip, and so did both excursions.

The Fijian Hotel occupies the whole of a large island in the lagoon. It had four dining-rooms, several restaurants for lunch, snack-bars, and buffets. There were facilities for all types of sports. You could be in and out of the lagoon all day or sailing at full tide in a glass-bottomed boat, walking the reef at low tide photographing the wonderful collection of fauna and flora. But the photo I treasure most was taken from the balcony of my room at six in the morning, of the sun coming up and shining through the palm trees on the beach.

The return journey was again forty-eight hours of travelling and again I went straight to bed, tired, yes, but I still do not know what jet lag is. I felt no sort of disorientation either way.

God Forms Light and Creates Darkness, He Makes Peace and Creates Evil . . . All with a Purpose

In chapter 4 I touch on the matter of accidents and make a suggestion that in no way fits in with modern thinking. The authorities are continuously striving to make variations designed to prevent accidents and, of course, fail because they are tackling not the cause but the symptoms, the signals of life that indicate that all is not well. Not well with what?

Elsewhere I have touched on ideas suggesting that unseen influences are constantly at work around us. To what end do these influences affect us? It would have been useless to try to consider these matters separately and in turn because they are so woven together in the pattern of life that to do justice we must start at the beginning, or as near to a beginning as is possible, and work our way through the logic of life to a conclusion in this chapter.

The Bible commences with the story of Adam and Eve—a beautiful allegory—and there have been many heated arguments between fundamentalists and those who accept Darwin's theory of evolution, which they feel is much more practical. Two intriguing references are made in the Bible that perhaps give us the opportunity to bring both sides together, i.e., it speaks of the children of God and the children of men. Much later on the Lord refers to Himself on the one hand as the "son of man" and on the other as "the son of God." Flesh on the one hand, Spirit on the other. Cain is made a fugitive and complains that his life would be in danger at the hands of others, which hardly fits in with the view that Adam and Eve were the first inhabitants of the world. The statement is also made that Cain took himself a wife of the "children of men."

Can it not be that men and women in the form of *Homo erectus* and *Homo sapiens* were indeed evolved animals but under the Divine Influence all the time and not chance? Chance could not function as a progressive force; the very nature of chance means that destructive elements exist which from time to time would inevitably destroy what progress had been made. The Divine Will prevents this and allows us to see progress in natural selection. So at some point God breathed into *Homo sapiens* and he became "a living soul," different from all other animals in his recognition of his otherworldliness and with the first stirrings of belief in a creative force. At the same time as he becomes aware of God, he also becomes aware of the possibility of life after death, another distinction between ourselves and animals. From there on, God or gods ruled the thoughts and lives of men and women. The need to worship is evident in all the early races of mankind wherever in the world they lived. The Ten Commandments of Judaism are closely related to the Code of Hammurabi, the Babylonian king circa 1792 to 1750 B.C., which was inscribed on a great stele of black basalt. It was taken for granted in those days that the earth, its produce, and its workers belonged to the gods. It was the distinctive attribute of the Hebrews that they recognised that there was only One God, Yahweh. All life was controlled by the need to worship. How different from the present day when the vast majority in the Western World recognise no gods at all except perhaps money. All along the line, however, the evidence of backsliding is significant, notably in the history of the Jewish race as given in the Old Testament. Continuously the prophets had to warn the population that it was ignoring God and pursuing its own aims and aspirations, very often though by resorting to their own made gods. I must restrain myself from digressing further because the point I wish to make is that while at one time the worship of God or of gods was automatic, there has been a gradual transition almost all over the world to a more relaxed and less obligatory form of worship. Indeed it is now so far advanced that in this country of Britain the majority of people do not believe in any God at all and therefore do not consider themselves under any obligation to obey anything but their natural instincts.

Nevertheless, everybody recognises that all sorts of unwanted events intrude into their lives, hence, that sad German song I quoted. And the general conception of life is that it is unjust, unfair, erratic, and subject to chance. As I have said elsewhere the words *chance, luck, accident,* and *coincidence* are all used to describe situations and events that we do not properly understand. The law of cause and effect states that "every cause has an effect and every effect is in itself a further cause." This is a sequence that has been evident from the beginning of life. Let us suppose that each one of us experiences, say, one hundred such sequences every day; in 365 that makes 36,500 for an average life of sixty years, i.e., 2,190,000 sequences in one person's life. Multiply that by an average of one thousand million people over a period of six thousand years, would twelve million, million, million be near enough? The fact, however, is that though the number of sequences of the law of cause and effect may run into millions and millions, the present world situation is understood by Omnipotent God. The Lord Christ knew very well what would transpire. Read Matthew chapter 24, which gives a word picture of the result of men and women following their own inclinations, which they call freedom. In fact they are in bondage to their own vices. But of course, if you do not believe there is a God and you do not subscribe to a moral code of living—if you do not

103

believe there is anything other than this life—then logic says you can and should do as you please. Get the most you can, while you can, for there is nothing after death. The curious thing is that very few people can go all the way and ride roughshod over others. People stop short of hurting others. What holds them back? Some sense of decency seems to have been inbred over the years so that drunkards are not necessarily rapists or child abusers or thieves or et cetera, et cetera. Those few homosexuals I have come upon have been quite nice, admirable people, but they will argue their case vehemently and always *objectively*. By that I mean that their case depends on the practical advantages they see in the flesh, while ignoring the *subjective* arguments of ethics based on spiritual values. Such spiritual values are to such people unrewarding. But God is not mocked; every licence taken by man in this life has to be paid for, not immediately but in due course. One other factor is the inability of people to blame themselves. They put the blame on others or on inanimate objects before they consider themselves to be at fault; so unless a person is earnestly seeking truth, the cause of misadventures escapes them. Let me reiterate a fundamental point made at the end of chapter 6. God created men and women, He blessed them and said "Be fruitful and multiply." That might seem to suggest that intercourse between man and woman can be promiscuous. How is it then that even in so-called primitive cultures there are taboos inhibiting not only promiscuity but setting well-defined standards for intercourse between man and wife. May I draw your attention again to the book of Leviticus, where you will read that men should refrain from going with their wives for several days before the menstrual period, during the periods, and for a few days after. This leaves seven to ten days when intercourse should take place—the so-called safe period. Condoms and pills are therefore not necessary for family planning. Self-discipline on the part of the man would be just as effective, and self-discipline in one direction would help towards self-discipline in other respects. But the safe period is in fact a safe period in another vital respect, and was and is the reason for the limitations, because one of the many functions of blood is to enable the body to deal with impurities, and the strictures and taboos are there to prevent the new birth from being contaminated by the impurities in the mother's blood. No criticism of the mother is intended; it is a bodily function.

In passing let us observe that the primitive races have obeyed their taboos much more successfully than other races have obeyed their laws.

How arrogant is mankind! Has not the potter full rights over the pot he creates? Has not God the "copyright" on His creation? We disobey and then complain about the results, yet we have been warned.

Deuteronomy 5, verses 9 and 10:

> . . . for I the Lord thy God am a jealous God, visiting the iniquity of the fathers upon the children unto the third and fourth generation of them that hate me.
> And showing mercy upon thousands of them that love me, and keep my commandments.

What repercussions are probable from today's practices of fertilising female eggs by outside donors of sperm or by interfering with genes? At the moment mankind sees only through rose-coloured spectacles, and when the adverse effects begin to show up men will not look back and blame themselves, oh, no. Obviously those who do not believe in God cannot be expected to obey His commandments: that is what we are here to learn.

So, at last, we have come to the vital question for which this book attempts to provide an answer.

In 1215 at the Fourth Lateran Council the bishops of the

then world wrestled with, among other things, the question of evil, and decided that God being good could not have created evil. Evil, they concluded, had somehow been generated by spontaneous combustion and God had been doing His best to combat it. This was a lie implanted by Satan to deceive, and how successful he has been. Just as successful as in the first instance of the devil proposing an untruth to Eve in the garden of Eden. Eve told the devil that God had said, "If you partake of the fruit of the tree of Knowledge of Good and Evil, thou shalt surely die." Satan said, "Hath God said that? Thou shalt not surely die," and Eve believed him.

Thus does the devil always put warped thoughts into the minds of men and women, and thus does he achieve his own nefarious and chaotic ends. Thus also have *all the religious denominations of the world* gone off the rails and remained derailed ever since. Because if you allow that evil was not created by God, then it has to be an agency of power apart from God, which is the lie that men have believed and still believe today. Despite the fact, therefore, that religious people are always singing and talking about the Omnipotence of God, they are always looking fearfully over their shoulders wondering what evil is going to come upon them unawares and wreck their lives. God is therefore not God, because He would be subservient to a greater power.

In conversation, from pulpits, over the media, there is the understanding that "you can't expect to go through life without some misadventure hitting you at times." And religious people as well as the worldly wise put "something by for a rainy day" and/or take out an insurance policy.

In the course of any conversation there will be almost constant reference to the hazards of life, meaning that unexpected, unwanted, and *unjust* events can upset things. Well, one has to admit that this can be so *but* not without meaning. There is meaning in all things. Nothing can happen that is uncontrolled or uncontrollable. Nothing can happen to us *by chance*. WHY?

Because Satan's lie is not true! God, the Creator of all things, God the Omnipotent, did create evil! Who planted the tree of Knowledge of Good and Evil in the garden of Eden? Who gave permission to the devil to tempt Job? Why did the Lord Christ before Pilate say, "Thou couldst have no power over me unless it were given thee from above"?

Isaiah, chapter 45, verses 5, 6, and 7 says:

I am the Lord, and there is none else, there is no God besides me: I girded thee though thou hast not known me;
    That they may know from the rising of the sun, and from the west, that there is none beside me, I am the Lord, and there is none else.
    I form the light and create darkness; I make peace and create evil; I, the Lord, do all these things.

Majestic, compelling, pulse-quickening words to some, a lot of nonsense to others. Evil is very difficult to define. Christian believers will read the story of the Crucifixion and say that it was evil, yet it resulted in the best possible good to mankind. If you lose an arm or a leg or an eye, one would say that was an evil result, yet the Lord Christ said it is better to lose a limb and enter into heaven than to keep whole and enter into perdition. That is why one may not be able to go through life without experiencing some "apparent" misfortune. It will not, however, be haphazard misfortune but misfortune under the control of the Divine Will for our good, not maybe of the body of flesh but of the soul. People are so often concerned with the flesh, and naturally so, that they overlook the soul. If we believe that God created evil then it is under His perfect will, and if it is His perfect will then should we not rejoice that He is so concerned for our (soul's) well-being.

So much in life can be seen to be in balanced opposition:

positive and negative; heat and cold; light and dark; coming and going; even good and evil. Why should we believe that God created all things and refuse, as a minister friend of mine did, to believe He created evil? It's not logical. There is, however, a much more impelling reason than mere logic, which dawned on me after my wife died and I was considering a holiday. Remember, I said I did not see much benefit in having a holiday without someone to share it with. Suddenly I realised that was just what God must have felt after He had created the world and all that is therein. What good is a perfect creation without someone with whom to share it? But if He created someone who could do no other than love Him because He had made them thus, what value would there be in that? Yet that is just what I have heard many say. "Why," they say, "could not God have made us so that we worshipped Him without having to suffer?"

But, surely, God would think, "I don't want men and women to love me because they can't help it; I want them to make a deliberate choice against other things and come willingly to me." And God made an important decision. He would make it possible for mankind to experience evil so that it could appreciate what good really was. After all, one could not know what light was without being able to realise the absence of it, i.e., dark. Then God must have thought, "If I let mankind dabble in evil, I must make it possible for them to turn back; I must therefore show them the way and be prepared to forgive them the direst wickedness." "Though your sins be as scarlet, they shall be white as snow, though they be red like crimson they shall be as wool" (Isa. 1:18). So God was prepared to underwrite His great plan by the sacrifice of His only begotten Son, Jesus Christ, and you can read it unfolding from Genesis to Revelation.

If, as the 'ologists all maintain—and I am not equipped to argue—life began on the seashore with the tides sweeping up the beaches and gradually causing life to adapt, then the same sort of thing is happening again. I have suggested a parallel between the magnetic effect of an electric current leaving as it does residual magnetism, and life with its recurring events each time having a residual effect on the subconscious. Let us change the imagery and see a mighty ocean of evil pounding the beaches of life and we mortals on the shore sometimes gently lapped by the waves, at other times submerged with great waves of evil. Our souls have to adapt to the varying situations, the law of cause and effect still being operative; but all the time there is progress in our ability to withstand or adapt to the successive waves of the evil ocean, so that we are moving by the grace of God towards the goal that He has set for each one of us.

In the early period life, it is said, gradually adapted to living on the land and in air without the sea being necessary. Could it not be that our souls gradually become so attuned to good lives that we no longer need and certainly no longer desire to be affected by evil. We turn away from it to God so that evil no longer has any influence over us; we desire only to worship our Creator in newness of spirit. We must change the analogy, for at this point evil, which has thrived on mankind's participation, will now no longer be of any use, and when a thing is not used it atrophies and dies.

I have listened to at least a hundred sermons on the story told by Jesus of the young man who demanded from his father what was due to him of his father's possessions and went away and "wasted his substance in riotous living." When he came to his senses he was overwhelmed with grief and returning sought his father's forgiveness. That forgiveness was given with rejoicing.

When we repent and seek forgiveness it is immediately given by our Father, with great rejoicing, for the Father knows that the son who has followed his own way and returned will not be tempted away again. This is the meaning of the story of the prodigal son. This is the meaning of evil in the world. When we have done our worst and, repentant, returned to God, He knows He has got us forever. We return to Him of our own free will, not because He has made us thus, but because we want Him above all other things. God knows He can then trust us and we shall not fail. We shall have passed through the refining fire, the dross burned off, the pure gold remaining.

To achieve partners like this with whom to share His magnificent creation, God has been willing to suffer with us, yea, much more than we have.

Then will come that great day when God shall be all in all; when at the name of Jesus, every knee shall bow, every tongue confess Him, King of Glory now.

Isaiah, speaking of Christ, says, "He shall see of the travail of His soul, and be satisfied" (Isa. 53:11).

This is the fulfilment of the plan of God, and it *will* come to pass, for the mouth of the Lord hath spoken it.

Then God shall wipe away all tears from the eyes.

Hallelujah.

Heaven is above.